THE
ANGEL
ORACLE

THE ANGEL ORACLE

AMBIKA WAUTERS

WORKING WITH THE ANGELS FOR
GUIDANCE, INSPIRATION AND LOVE

First published in Great Britain in 1995
This edition published by OH!
An imprint of Welbeck Publishing Group
20 Mortimer Street, London, W1T 3JW, UK
www.welbeckpublishing.com

British Library Cataloguing-in-Publication data available on request.

ISBN 978-1-80069-273-2

1 3 5 7 9 10 8 6 4 2

Printed in China

CONTENTS

Introduction 6

Chapter One Angels Past and Present 10

Chapter Two The Angel Cards 15

The Heaven of Form 17
The Archangels 20
The Guardian Angels 30
The Angel Princes 48

The Heaven of Creation 56
The Powers 60
The Virtues 66
The Dominions 72

The Heaven of Paradise 78
The Seraphim 82
The Cherubim 88
The Thrones 94

Chapter Three How to Use the Angel Cards 100

How to Prepare the Cards 100
Asking the Oracle Questions 101
Choosing a Card Spread 101
Interpretation of the Cards 102
Conclusion 110

Suggested Reading 111   Acknowledgements 112

INTRODUCTION

Blessed is the child of Light
Who doth seek his Heavenly Father,
For he shall have eternal life.
He that dwelleth in the secret place
Of the most High
Shall abide under the Shadow of the Almighty.
For He shall give his Angels charge over thee,
To keep thee in all thy ways.

THE GOSPEL OF THE ESSENES

Angels have been our link with the Divine Source – the ultimate Origin of all creation – since the beginning of our search into the mysteries of life and the nature of our existence. They are also an aspect of our relationship with the Source representing the total intention of goodness, purity and light.

THE ANGEL ORACLE is an opportunity to rekindle awareness of the bridge between our ordinary lives and the realm of the Divine. It comes out of many years of my experience in developing clairvoyance and intuition, using such divinatory tools as the I-Ching and the Runes. Though based on ancient archetypal symbols representing the essence of our nature, these cards also embrace a luminous presence which helps guide us towards a knowing and loving consciousness. I have attempted to distil that divinatory quality into an Oracle which offers a deep and abiding sense of Self and which shows us how the Divine works through us to help bring order and clarity into our lives.

THE ANGEL ORACLE arises out of a curiosity about angels and a sense of marvel and delight at how they complement our physical reality and help our lives unfold. Angels have been a part of my world since early child-hood, and with the reawakening of my 'angel consciousness' something deep inside me resonated with this awareness and affirmed the presence of angels in my life

I have been deeply moved and inspired by several new books about angels. The one which had the most profound influence on me, and which I describe in Chapter One, was *Talking with Angels* by Gitta Mallasz. After reading this I was left in no doubt that angels were not airy-fairy, nor to be dismissed as New Age creations. The certainty of the young people described in this book that angels were guiding and protecting them moved me beyond words.

After reading a good few books on the subject I started to keep a journal of the ways in which angels worked in my life. I was startled and then amazed by the constant flood of inspiration and guidance that was there for me whenever I tuned into it. I learned to differentiate my own personal Guardian Angel from those who guided me to create THE ANGEL ORACLE.

As my awareness of angels developed, I began to notice them everywhere I looked. They were carved on secular buildings as well as their more obvious place in old churches. I found them on cash registers in a health food shop, and displayed on the front of a national magazine. I turned my bedroom into what I called my 'Angelorium' and put beautiful pictures of angels on the walls. Angel awareness became a full-time reality for me. I even started painting and sculpting angels afresh, but now with deep delight. I started to meet wonderfully conscious people who had also had experiences with angels. Many of them are truly loving and kind and have deeply enriched my life.

I use the angel cards to help me in a variety of different situations. I may want insight into a problem which I am uncertain how to handle, or I may wish to know which choice is right for my greatest joy and highest good. In calling on them I ask the angels to reveal their love and guidance through the card deck. They offer me assistance with my work, my relationships and even with my finances. They remind me that when I let go of my ego they act as supports and guides through my fears or indecisions. I have learned to trust that they know more than my small mind could ever cope with knowing. Through the cards they reveal trends and events to me which invariably unfold just as predicted.

Awareness of the angels grows the more we open ourselves and trust in their power to make our lives happier and more joyful. It was the angels who helped me realize when it was time to play and to give up struggling with writing, or with anything else for that matter. Where I used to endure extended bouts of guilt over not doing enough work, I suddenly found it much easier to manage my time efficiently so that I could write, study, see clients and still have the opportunity to play. Angels constantly teach me to love myself unconditionally, as they love me. This love extends beyond any judgements I might cherish about my worth or lack of it. The angels have guided me with gentleness and humour to love and accept myself, no matter what.

Angels can become part of your reality too. It takes an open heart and a gentle and non-judgemental mind to allow their grace to fill your life. As you begin to acquaint yourself with the different types of angelic guidance offered in THE ANGEL ORACLE, perhaps you will sense their sweet and friendly nature and their generous, guiding spirits. They are here to provide ways in which you can find your joy and ease in life. They offer sustenance and comfort when you find yourself bereft or alone. They are a symbolic shoulder for you to lean on when you feel down or times are hard. More than anything, they bring you the unconditional love and light of the Source.

It is my hope and intention that, in acquainting yourself with the angels in THE ANGEL ORACLE, you can find these qualities within yourself and own the projection of angels as part of your own Divine Nature: in short, that you discover your own angelic qualities. I also hope that you become comfortable with the Divine assistance available in coming to solutions and answers to whatever you seek in life.

I feel that most of us with everyday, ordinary lives may not have had any direct experience of angels. However, that does not mean they are not around; quite the contrary. They are working, active and present, and awaiting the shift in our consciousness which will enable us to touch their realm of existence. It is up to us to open ourselves to their vibration and let their love flow into our lives. We can pray to our angels for help and guidance and offer them thanks for the good they bring us. We can also ask specific angels to help us find the solutions and answers to our particular problems.

There is no one I know who could not use a little more help in today's uncertain world. Relationships are put under a great deal of strain as we rapidly move away from simplicity, striving for more money, success, qualifications, and so on. Many of us have lost contact with our guiding and protecting angels. We can re-establish this contact easily and with grace when we make the simple choice to open ourselves to their guiding light, which has been freely offered us. What is asked of us is to give up our old, stale scripts about how life has to be and how we should live it.

When we relinquish some of our preconceived ideas, we have a very real chance of clearing the way for angels to enter our lives and open our hearts. We all have a guiding angel who watches over us and protects us. We have the possibility of saying 'hello' and 'thank you' more often than we realize. This angel is always there for us. Have you ever had the feeling that you were stopped from having a serious accident, or found yourself doing the right thing at the right time, even saying the right and most comforting words to help a friend in pain? These all come about with the help of the angels.

Trust your Higher Self to put you in touch with the angels. You can use the angel cards to help you find answers to questions about your life. You can also use them as a stepping-stone to get better acquainted with the angels. They want you to get to know them and trust them. Being open to them is really opening yourself to your highest good and greatest joy. They await your conscious recognition of them. They can offer each of us the best help, counsel, guidance and protection we could possibly need in life. The more responsibility we take as co-creators of the universe the more the angels help raise our consciousness to a level we know as bliss. They are there to sing to us and help us find our joy in the here and now, in our physical bodies, on the planet, wherever we may be.

THE ANGEL ORACLE was developed over the past few years, inspired by the angels who helped me construct it for my own guidance and assistance. I am delighted to share it with you, and I trust it shows you possibilities which are positive and enlightening, so that you may live your truth, find love and make your path simple and easy.

Chapter One

ANGELS PAST AND PRESENT

The soul at its highest is found like God, but an angel gives a closer idea of Him. That is all an angel is: an idea of God.

MEISTER ECKHART, SERMONS

Angels are as close to the Divine as we can get. Our knowledge of them comes from written descriptions of people's luminous and mystical experiences. They have appeared in the records of civilization marking events where tremendous shifts in human consciousness have occurred. For instance, we see angels appearing to men and women whose destinies were to lead others towards greater awareness and moral responsibility.

We have vast quantities of literature about the angels' help and assistance to the Jews of the Old Testament in their struggle for freedom. Hebrew literature has a firm understanding about the nature of the love and grace the angels confer upon humanity. Angels are called Malach in Hebrew. The stories of the angel visiting Abraham to intervene on Isaac's behalf or of the angels helping Daniel and protecting Shadrach, Meshach and Abednego in the burning fiery furnace are favourite Biblical tales.

The Book of Revelation and the Apocrypha describe angels as the Lord's messengers, used to reveal his love for mankind. St Luke tells of the angel Gabriel's annunciation of Christ's coming to Mary. The word angel derives from the Greek word angeloi, which means, in fact, messenger. Angels are prominent throughout the Koran and have a significant place in the sacred Islamic texts. The Koran tells how Gabriel carried Muhammed up to Heaven one starlit night and dictated the entire Book to him. This is honoured as a holy event which marks the celestial inauguration of an ethical and sacred code to all who follow Islam.

Three of the main religions of modern civilization have thus ordained and blessed the presence of angels. We need only look at the ancient writings which are the backbone and foundation of these religions to understand the extent to which angels acted as revelatory messengers of God in the past. How these teachings, with their many miracles, can be seen to relate to our everyday understanding now is as a backdrop for our present-day experience with these wondrous creatures of light. We hope that conventional religious attitudes about angels will not discourage you from opening yourself to a possibility of gaining insight and knowledge into the love and healing they can offer each of us.

Angels, in fact, belong to all mankind, not to any particular religion. They can serve us as agents for personal growth and spiritual evolution. All you need to do is to allow the angels space in your life to create the spiritual context in which to develop a capacity to love and to be loved.

Angels can have an active place in our lives because we need them to help us in our relationship to the Source. As well, they give us protection and guidance and they can help us fulfil our creative potential by making our way easy and smooth. They help by removing obstacles to our well-being and happiness. In modern times two strongly influential thinkers, Emanuel Swedenborg and Rudolf Steiner, have helped to shift our awareness of angels from a religious to a humanistic view. Emanuel Swedenborg was a Swedish philosopher who lived in the eighteenth century. He had profound mystical experiences during which, he attests, he was taken into the realm of Heaven and was witness to the heavenly hierarchies. He described in his writings the perfect love and harmony of the angelic kingdom. He told of angels having homes and living in perfect harmony and peace. Angels, of course, had a blissful existence. According to Swedenborg they married and co-habited and their lives were not dissimilar to our own, except that they lived without strife or conflict and never struggled for anything. This is, by any standard, a lovely vision of Heaven and something we can aspire to transpose to our earthly existence.

Swedenborg described the acts of love and charity which the angels performed. He said they were never more blissful than when they were teaching or offering guidance and care: 'They are the image of the Lord, thus do they love their neighbour more than themselves, and for this reason, heaven is heaven.'

Around the turn of the present century Rudolf Steiner, a German scientist and philosopher, studied all forms of esoteric sciences. He had a deep love and understanding of the angels. Steiner understood the purpose of angels as being that of spiritual teachers helping mankind achieve a higher level of spirituality and inner development. He said that the more we evolved as spiritual beings the more we connected with the angelic realms. He felt, for instance, that the archangel Michael was the guiding angel of our New Age and would help lead mankind out of the chaotic and dispirited state into which it had sunk, towards an age of great light and spiritual consciousness.

An important part of Steiner's writings is his description of how angels communicate with us. He said that this was through images. According to Steiner we need to develop imagination and intuition in order to decode what the angels desire to reveal to us. In fact, the work we can do with angels has the result of releasing our negativity and unlocking our mind-sets about physical reality. This helps us to develop our intuitive thinking and to expand our creative capacity. Meditating on the angelic clears negative thought-patterns so that we are open to receive the celestial messages.

These messages are channelled through the right hemisphere of the brain. This hemisphere has a synthetic function in assessing information, which means that it brings information together and forms images of it. It is the part of the brain which receives stimulation in the form of music, colour and touch. It works from images and symbols, so that conclusions, rather than results, take on a metaphoric quality. It is discriminating rather than judgemental. It is inclusive as opposed to exclusive: while the left hemisphere divides and breaks down information through analytic processes, the right one collates information into a cohesive and comprehensive pattern.

We gain access to the angelic images we receive through the right hemisphere of the brain. That is why it is important to find pleasure and delight in art, music and dance as well as touch. It opens us up to the part of us that reaches the Source through direct experience. Actually, what we seek is balance between the hemispheres, to be able to use our brain to its full capacity.

Steiner felt that each picture we were given was part of an encoded vision of our ultimate happinesss. The more we developed our intuition, the more we would be able to extrapolate this information, make clear choices and thus live healthy and orderly lives, serving our highest good at all times and helping humanity to evolve. Steiner felt that the purpose of angelic teaching was threefold. He felt that each person would find their own link with divinity; each person would come to live in freedom, honouring the Divine Source within themselves and within their fellow humans.

In her book *Talking with Angels*, which I mentioned in the Introduction, Gitta Mallasz offers us an extraordinary view of how angels transformed the lives of four young people, including herself, the only one to survive, who hid in a small village in Hungary during World War II. The particularly striking feature of the book is that it describes the living hell to which these people were submitted and the inner peace and tranquillity they were able to achieve because of their regular contact with the angels. This contact was channelled through a session with one of the four on a weekly basis for eighteen months. It provided their spiritual sustenance through a time of nearly total global despair. Gitta Mallasz, now elderly, lives in France and occasionally broadcasts radio talks on the subject of angels.

The American writer Terry Lynn Taylor writes about angels in a way which takes the religious overtones away and instead shows us the love and light they are so eager to offer us. Her books take us to the core of why we look to angels for guidance and protection. She quite simply states that they are here to bring us our joy. Gustav Davidson, another modern writer, was a scholar whose interest in angels was profound. He wrote a Dictionary of Angels which gives us a wealth of knowledge and information about these heavenly beings. His interest spanned many years of research. We are deeply indebted to him for his prodigious research into a subject which gave him great joy. He also helped remove the purely religious associations from angels and bring them into the light of everyday consciousness. He hoped that anyone who enjoyed knowing about angels would find his work a handy and useful guide.

The angels offer us the opportunity to love our Selves. They bring us to the very essence of our lives by teaching us that when we love ourselves we follow our highest truth. They help us to mature into responsible and loving people who can live from a place of serenity and peace. They assist us in finding who we really are in the depths of our being, as well as how to live as creative, whole people. Nearly all the modern literature on angels offers us this perspective, illuminating the essence of what angels have to share with us in our ordinary, everyday lives.

Dr H. C. Moolenburgh of Holland has written two books about people's experiences with angels. There are many other accounts of people sharing their personal encounters with angels and describing how they were helped. Some are miraculous and extraordinary, others are simple, and reveal how easily angels can come into our lives when we are open to their love, wisdom and guidance.

Belief in angels is clearly a personal choice. They inhabit the realm of the invisible. Their actions, however, are experienced in the form of energy which manifests itself physically and expresses itself as living reality. How do we know if something is real? We see the results of its power. When a car avoids hitting a child at the last instant, or help for a problem turns up out of nowhere, I feel certain that we are dealing with the angelic. Inspiration comes from a higher place than our rational, conscious minds can offer. We can use our analytical, left hemisphere brain to assess our experiences, but when we start to open our minds to another possibility, the possibility of a reality that is enhanced with angelic guidance and love, we may find help when we are distressed, and answers to problems that seem unfathomable. At such a moment we begin to let in the beauty of the angels.

Information about the angels may be useful but it is not necessary for making contact with them. The more you can open yourself to experiencing the angels in your life the more familiar you will become with them. Books can help us share in other people's experiences, but they are no substitute for our own personal awareness. In truth, the angels ask us to develop our intuitive gifts so that we can better understand what they hope to teach us. When you begin to trust your heart and to honour all your feelings as legitimate expressions of yourself, then the angels can reach your mind and heart faster. This means that you trust yourself and, first and foremost, respect your experience. Often it is simple people with very uncomplicated experiences who meet the angels easily. So try to move away momentarily from your rational, left-brain way of looking at the world, and be willing to open your senses and your intuition to another way of perceiving which allows you to tap into the wonders of universal consciousness. The love of the angels and the joy of pure being are waiting for you.

Chapter Two

THE ANGEL CARDS

Angels are the economy of the visible world. I consider them
as the real cause of motion, light and life, and of those elementary
principles of the physical universe, which, in their development to
our senses, suggest to us the notion of cause and effect and of
what are called the laws of nature.

CARDINAL NEWMAN

This introduction to the angel cards comprises a description of the angels and their heavenly and earthly functions. The cards have been designed to correspond with the three hierarchies of Heaven: the Heaven of Form, which relates to our everyday, material life; the Heaven of Creation, which exalts human affairs and relationships and the way humankind deals with fellow humans; and the Heaven of Paradise, which shows us how we can participate as co-creators of the Universe together with the Source. The cards of the three Heavens can be recognized by their different border decoration. To help you to get to know the angel cards I would like to suggest that you sort them out into the three hierarchies, following the order given in this chapter, and begin to familiarize yourself with them. Your first impressions are important. Read the affirmation on each card – the essence of the angel and its meaning – and study its image. Trust your instincts about the cards and then read about them. This way your own impressions will stand out and be significant to you, and the cards will be an excellent divinatory tool for you.

Each level of Heaven has three kinds of angel. The Heaven of Form contains the protection and love of the Archangels. Our personal Guardian Angels and the Angel Princes who rule over specific geographical locations also inhabit this realm. The Heaven of Creation contains the tender and merciful energies of the Powers, Virtues and Dominions. These are the angels who directly affect the spiritual nature of human relationships. They offer us such qualities as peace, serenity, and harmony. They also help us to accept reconciliation and mercy in our lives and they aid us in finding forgiveness in our hearts. The Heaven of Paradise holds the glorious and powerful energies of the Seraphim, Cherubim and Thrones. These are the angels of love, wisdom and glory.

The hierarchy of Heaven is defined by the degree of love and awareness within each realm. Just as we evolve spiritually on the earth plane, so angels also evolve from one level to another, expanding their consciousness and love. They come closer to the Source through love and charity. Acting as God's messengers, they bring the universal light of love into the consciousness of all beings. They serve the Source by helping us evolve into worthy beings; creatures of light and love.

When we use the angel cards as an oracle we are calling on the combined energies and awareness of all the Heavens. We are asking the entire heavenly hierarchy to assist us in finding solutions to our problems and giving us insight into our lives and the emotional and spiritual processes we may be undergoing. The angels are there to help us reconnect with the Source. They are at our disposal and may be called upon at any time.

THE ANGEL ORACLE does not pretend to have the answers to all your problems. It can, however, offer you a tool for reaching up to touch the guidance and love of our divine friends. As you look through the cards and become familiar with the qualities of the different angels, you may be struck by the high level of love they can bring to us. Each level of Heaven has its own specific function. Depending upon your own special need for guidance and help, look to see which angels resonate with your problem or particular issues.

At different times throughout your development you may be calling on different angels for help and guidance. If your problems revolve around material issues, such as how to find your way in the world or how to make a living doing something which gives you pleasure and joy, you might seek the assistance of one of the Archangels or your Guardian Angel. If, on the other hand, your particular issues are focused on relationships and involve your role with different people or one specific person you may find yourself drawing the angel cards from the Heaven of Creation.

The hierarchies of Heaven offer you a gauge with which to measure your own level of awareness and capacity for spirituality. Trust that as you expand your faith in angels they will help you to reach higher levels of love and joy.

THE HEAVEN OF FORM

The Heaven of Form is the first of the three levels of Heaven, and the angels of this realm, the Archangels, Guardians and Angel Princes, are those closest to mankind. They are our primary contact with the angelic realms and offer us both personal and transpersonal assistance in bringing order and happiness into our lives. Their purpose is to help us realize that the Divine is in everyone and everything around us. They provide the spirit of love and protection which is vital to the nourishment of our souls on this earthly plane. Without a spiritual context within which to hold our worldly experiences we would be bereft. The more we choose love in our lives the more we align with the heavenly realms.

The Archangels

The Archangels are messengers from the Divine to mankind. They offer spiritual sustenance and inspiration. They provide us with revelation and supply all the tools we need for our spiritual development. They offer us the highest quality of assistance and heavenly love for use in our daily lives. We are given their light and strength to guide us back to the power within ourselves through which we can become co-creators of the universe together with the Source. They are, in effect, protectors of humankind and have specific functions which aid the collective and universal spirit of the human race.

Through their ability to penetrate material substance, archangels transform earth energy and remind us of the limitations of our small minds. They show us the boundless reality of the Divine. When we accept their presence we are inviting miracles into our lives. Throughout the ages people have turned to the Archangels for succour and support. An ancient Jewish prayer invokes their aid:

> *To God Almighty,*
> *The Lord of Israel,*
> *May Michael be at my right hand,*
> *Gabriel at my left hand,*
> *Before me Raphael and*
> *Behind me Uriel,*
> *And above me the Divine Presence of God.*

The Guardian Angels

While the Archangels reign over the whole of mankind, the Guardian Angels attach themselves to individuals. It is the Guardian Angels who watch over individuals' spiritual growth throughout their lives and protect and defend their souls. Each angel may have been with a particular soul for many lifetimes, helping that individual to piece together the lessons of each lifetime until, at last, it knows it is one with God. That knowing is called enlightenment.

Our Guardian Angel blesses everything that we do to nurture our spirit's welfare. It could be an exacting spiritual practice which gives peace or serenity; it could be as simple as encouraging us to go to the beach and play Frisbee. Childish fun and playfulness can be as satisfying to the soul as hours of meditation or self-help therapies.

In THE ANGEL ORACLE the Guardian Angels represent the different stages of development we pass through in our lives. They stand as a symbol for the passages we all make as we mature and develop along our path. We can tap into these Guardians for guidance and help whenever we are stuck or blocked in our lives. They love and cherish us unconditionally. They are available for help at any time we open ourselves to accept their Divine presence.

In the last century Alexander Carmichael found a beautiful prayer to a Guardian Angel in the Outer Isles of Scotland:

The Guardian Angel

Thou angel of God who hast charge of me
From the dear Father of mercifulness,
To the shepherding King of the fold of the saints
To make round about me this night,

Drive from me every temptation and danger,
Surround me on the sea of unrighteousness,
And in the narrows, crooks and straits,
Keep thou my coracle, keep it always.

Be thou a bright flame before me,
Be thou a guiding star above me,
Be thou a smooth path below me,
And be a kindly shepherd behind me,

Today, tonight and forever.
I am tired and I a stranger,
Lead thou me to the land of angels;
For it is time to go home
To the court of Christ, to the peace of Heaven.

The Angel Princes

The Angel Princes are the protectors, helpers and guides of races, nations and towns. They are spoken of in the Bible as having a strong and powerful influence on the destiny of great masses of people. They represent the collective spirit of different types of humanity and their combined presence amounts to the spirit of a place. A lovely quote which well describes the Angel Prince is a line from Wallace Stevens's poem *Angels surrounded by Paysan:*

Yet I am the necessary angel of earth,
Since, in my sight, you see the earth again....

The Angel Princes help mankind by giving blessings and guidance where the welfare of nations is involved. These spirits are there to help mankind resolve those major affairs which influence the fates of the multitude. The Angel Princes strive to link the decisions of rulers with universal concepts of truth and justice.

In THE ANGEL ORACLE the Angel Princes will be used to denote the four directions of the compass, the four elements in nature and the four psychological functions which make up the conscious mind: thinking, feeling, sensation and intuition. In this way the Angel Princes relate directly to every one of us and to our lives. They focus on the psychological aspects of the three-dimensional world, and can assist us in understanding the essence of our situations.

The Archangel
METATRON

The Archangel **METATRON**
I AM UNITED WITH THE SOURCE OF ALL
GOODNESS, LOVE AND CREATIVITY

Metatron appears as the most earthly of Archangels, as he was once a wise and virtuous man whom God took up into Heaven. He is richly attired and holds a pen in one hand as he records our deeds in the Book of Life. He has the ability to help us know the true measure of things.

ANGELIC REALM
Archangel of the Heaven of Form

HEAVENLY FUNCTION
Recorder of the *Book of Life* and scribe for all our deeds

GIFTS FOR EARTH
He helps us to find the proper measure for all we do;
he acts as witness to the good we do and the love we give; he helps
us realize our potential as loving and worthwhile human beings

Metatron is the only angel within the heavenly spheres who was once human. He was known as Enoch and was the seventh Patriarch after Adam. It was written that he 'walked with God' and was taken up into Heaven where he was made an Archangel. There is speculation in Jewish scripture that he is the Shekinah, the angel who led the children of Israel out of the wilderness. It is thought too that it was Metatron who stopped Abraham from sacrificing his son Isaac to God.

Metatron is also known as the first and last of the Archangels and is variously called the Chancellor of Heaven, the Angel of the Covenant and the King of the Angels. His heavenly function is to supervise the recording of all our deeds in the *Book of Life*.

He is charged with sustaining human life and acts as the bridge between the Divine and mankind. We can seek counsel from him by asking him to help us find the proper measure for every action we take in our lives. At one level this means helping us find the balance between what we give out and what we keep for ourselves. This enables us to maintain well-defined boundaries and thus keep a clear sense of self, so necessary if we are to succeed in fulfilling our potential within the world of form.

Metatron can help us find the proper measure in love, work and recreation so that we live balanced, healthy lives, rich in harmony and serenity. He will also be a witness to the good we do, perhaps those acts of love or kindness not recognized by others. He can also help us when we have put effort and toil into making something work, whatever it is: it could be anything from trying to make a relationship work, losing weight, or giving up an addictive or damaging habit, to throwing ourselves fully into a cause or team effort.

We can pray to The Archangel Metatron to guide our efforts and to help us find the right measure for our output and activities. We can ask Metatron in our meditation to assist us in knowing when 'enough is enough', or when we need to do more for ourselves or others.

The Archangel

MICHAEL

The Archangel **MICHAEL**
I STAND FOR JUSTICE AND TRUTH.
I LIVE FROM MY INTEGRITY

Michael is the warrior whose light triumphs over the darkness of negativity. He is depicted carrying scales to weigh the souls on Judgement Day, as well as a sword to subdue Satan and the powers of darkness. He is seen slaying the dragon. The legend of St George derives directly from him.

ANGELIC REALM
Archangel of the Heaven of Form

HEAVENLY FUNCTION
Commander-in-chief of the Heavenly Armies

GIFTS FOR EARTH
He can help us to stand strong in the face of adversity;
resolve our personal negativities;
find strength when we are alone or feeling like outsiders

Michael's name translates from the Hebrew as 'Look Like God'. He is the Archangel we invoke in our battle against negativity. He helps us find the light within ourselves. Historically he is the protector of both Israel and the Catholic Church. He is the patron saint of policemen, soldiers and small children and also watches over pilgrims and strangers. He is the fiery warrior, Prince of the Heavenly Armies, who fights for right and justice and gives guidance to all those who find themselves in dire straits. Michael is also the bringer of patience and happiness.

He is associated with the element of fire, which symbolizes the burning away of what is transient so that only the pure and essential light may shine forth. He is called the benevolent Angel of Death because he brings us deliverance and immortality. He is the Angel of the Final Reckoning and Weigher of Souls.

Michael is considered the greatest of all angels in the Jewish, Christian and Islamic religions. He is known variously as Holder of the Keys of Heaven and Chief of the Archangels, Prince of the Presence, Angel of Repentance, Righteousness, Mercy and Sanctification, Angelic Prince of Israel, Guardian of Jacob, and Angel of the Burning Bush. He is a tireless champion of good, and always supports the underdog. Michael rules over the lonely struggler; he is always lending a hand to help alleviate strife and trouble.

We can pray to Michael to help us conquer our negativity. Whenever we become stuck he can assist us in lifting our spirit towards a more enduring vision of life. He is there to guide and protect us against injustice and to help us open ourselves to what is eternal and lasting. We can ask him to help us in any situation where we feel overwhelmed or alone and in need of support.

— ✳ —

The Archangel
GABRIEL

The Archangel **GABRIEL**
I AM MADE WHOLE BY THE MESSAGE OF LOVE,
BROTHERHOOD AND FREEDOM

Gabriel is depicted holding a lily, which stands for purity and truth. He is sometimes seen with an ink-well and quill, symbolizing his function as the heavenly communicator of the Word of God. He can also be seen holding a golden chalice strongly reminiscent of the Grail.

ANGELIC REALM
Archangel of the Heaven of Form

ANGELIC FUNCTION
To stand for truth and deliver the word of God

GIFTS FOR EARTH
He can help us to express our truth openly and honestly;
respect and honour our individuality;
listen to our intuition and inner voice

Traditionally Gabriel is the messenger of the Word of God. His name means 'God is my Strength'. He announces the mystery of incarnation to all souls before they are born and he instructs us all as to what our talents and tasks in this world will be. He is the patron saint of small children and he looks after and nourishes the child in each of us, a child who may be arrested in growth or wounded and in need of love. He guides us to release our inner child with words of tenderness and love. His guiding hand is always there to protect what is natural and pure within us.

All religions honour Gabriel as the most powerful messenger of the Source. He never tires of delivering the Word of God to those who will listen and honour the Source within themselves. He is known as the Chief Ambassador to Humanity, the Angel of Revelation, the Bringer of Good News, Judgement and Mercy. He is the Angel of Joy, and the Spirit of Truth.

Gabriel helps us to find the wisdom in our physical bodies and to know our personal truths. He respects the absolute individuality of each person. He can assist us to live our truths faithfully, honouring our talents and gifts. He can help us find the courage to live from the deep knowledge within ourselves which respects our God-given abilities. Gabriel can also help us succeed in developing our individual gifts and fully expressing ourselves.

Gabriel's quintessential gift to us is to nurture our strength and our conviction that we are each making a valuable contribution to the spiritual development of humanity simply by being who we are. He is available to help us ascertain the truth in situations where there is conflict between what we know to be right and what is being represented as truth. He helps us to see what is real for us in every situation where our insight and intuition are called upon to direct and guide us. Gabriel lights the way to the truth within our hearts, and helps us to see what is the right path for us to follow for our highest good and greatest joy.

— ✳ —

The Archangel

RAPHAEL

The Archangel **RAPHAEL**
I AM STRENGTHENED AND HEALED
BY THE POWER OF DIVINE LOVE

Raphael is seen walking with a staff or caduceus entwined with a snake, symbolizing healing. He carries a water gourd and in front of him leaps the curative fish. He is often shown with his right forefinger pointing up towards Heaven in a gesture of reassurance and hope, reminding us where true healing comes from.

ANGELIC REALM
Archangel of the Heaven of Form

HEAVENLY FUNCTION
Angel of healing through joy

GIFTS FOR EARTH
He can help us to seek the gift of healing;
he shows us ways to heal ourselves;
he helps us find the healing in nature and universal energy

Raphael is responsible for healing the earth and its inhabitants. He is credited with healing Abraham after he was circumcised and is the angel who handed Moses a book of all the herbs which exist to heal maladies. The Book of Tobias in the Old Testament relates how Raphael healed Tobias's father of blindness with an ointment made from the burned gall-bladder of a large fish. Raphael is variously known as the Overseer of the Evening Winds, Guardian of the Tree of Life in the Garden of Eden, Angel of Repentance, Prayer, Love, Joy and Light. He is the Angel of Healing, Science and Knowledge. He is also called the Angel of Providence who watches over all humanity.

His name means 'Divine Healer' or 'God Heals'. Raphael is the spiritual source behind all cures, and as a messenger of Divine Providence he brings healing to all who seek wholeness. He stands for the definitive, essential cure to all ills, which is the return to the Source. Raphael assists us to heal our bodies, minds and hearts. He helps us to achieve health and wholeness. He offers to help all who suffer and need healing, and whenever possible alleviates pain. When we open our hearts to healing, Raphael guides us to the healers, therapists and counsellors who do their best to help us. As we take more responsibility for our own healing he encourages the healer within each of us who knows what is best for our health and vitality.

He can help us to see the healing lessons in illness and to understand what suffering can teach us about ourselves. When we choose a healthy path his spirit guides us to attain maximum health.

As we transform our wounded minds and hearts we come close to touching Raphael's wings and gaining access to his Divine gifts. He is always available to guide us to wholeness and harmony. We need only wish it for ourselves.

— ✳ —

The Archangel

URIEL

The Archangel **URIEL**
DIVINE LIGHT SHINES FROM WITHIN.
I AM ETERNALLY RADIANT, LOVING AND WISE

Uriel is the Regent of the Sun and is the most radiant of the Archangels. He is shown with a flame in his open hand. He also rules over thunder and terror. Uriel is sometimes seen with a book at his feet, signifying the book he gave to Adam with all the medicinal herbs in it.

ANGELIC REALM
Archangel of the Heaven of Form

HEAVENLY FUNCTION
To bring us the light of the knowledge of God

GIFTS FOR EARTH
He can help us to acknowledge the Light within all people;
find knowledge to help and to heal;
interpret and decode our inner voice

Uriel, whose name means 'Light of God', is the angel who brings humankind knowledge and understanding of the Divine. He is the most radiant of angels and has been depicted descending from heaven on a fiery chariot drawn by white horses.

He has been variously called the Flame of God, Angel of the Presence, and Angel of Salvation. He is also known as the Prince of Light and interpreter of prophecies. It was Uriel whom God sent to Noah to warn him of the deluge. The Bible also tells how Uriel descended into the Garden of Eden on a sunbeam and stood at its gate with a fiery sword. He is also the angel who watches over thunder and terror. As the Angel of Repentance he can help us to understand the laws of karma, which, put very simply, mean that we reap what we sow. Uriel also helps us understand how Divine mercy works and brings us awareness that we are all cherished by God's love.

He is supposed to be the most sharp-sighted of all the angels. He is often represented with the flame of knowledge in his open hand, which mankind can draw upon for health and welfare. If this knowledge is abused then it is Uriel who delivers Divine retribution. Uriel helps us understand why all things are as they are. He helps us trust in the Divine plan so that when things appear to be going wrong we can know that ultimately they are for the highest good and greatest joy.

Uriel helps us interpret our inner voice and our dreams. He guides us towards understanding our essential nature and towards taking more responsibility for our lives. With his guidance we have the possibility of fulfilling our potential as creative spirits. Uriel helps us to find our inner light and to become as radiant as the sun when we express the fullness of the love and beauty within ourselves.

— ✶ —

The Guardian Angel of

CHILDREN

The Guardian Angel of **CHILDREN**
I HONOUR THE PRECIOUS CHILD WITHIN ME.
I NOURISH AND CHERISH ALL NEW BEGINNINGS

This beautiful angel guards and protects all that is new and young in life, especially new-born babies. It watches over anything that is beginning to grow and that needs extra nourishment, gentleness and care.

ANGELIC REALM
Angel of the Heaven of Form

ANGELIC FUNCTION
To guard and protect all children

GIFTS FOR EARTH
It can help you to protect the child within who longs to feel
safe and loved; look after all new beginnings in your life;
honour what is young and fresh in your life

The protective angel who watches over all new souls incarnated into earthly life, this angel helps mothers and babies at births. It also guides and protects all those who help to manage young babies and children. Every new baby and young person is blessed, protected and cherished by its Guardian Angel.

This angel also assists at any new beginnings, of new projects or relationships. It protects whatever is fresh and vulnerable, helping to nurture and sustain what is young so that it can grow strong and resilient. Whatever is new in your life can be blessed by the loving and vigilant care offered by this angel.

By praying to The Guardian Angel of Children we can give thanks and rejoice in the miracle of new life. We can ask for guidance and protection for all that is young and tender within us. We can ask this blessing for our families, friends, and those we associate with in our jobs, as well as others with whom we come into contact on a daily basis. All that is young and tender in us, vulnerable or in need of care, deserves a blessing from this special Guardian Angel. It will help to protect what is innocent and pure in us as well. That inner child who longs for acceptance and cherishing is acknowledged by your Guardian Angel.

The Guardian Angel of Children can help us to touch the child in us who is lonely or unloved. It can also help us to heal deep wounds where there has been a scarcity of love, or even abuse. We can ask this Guardian Angel to help us release pain, sorrow and upsetting memories from our past and to find healing for our spirit. This angel offers the protection that all new beginnings require to grow and flourish. It gives us the nurturing we need to acquire our strength and feel our stability in new situations. It allows the tender blooms of all new beginnings to root and take hold in solid ground.

— ✶ —

The Guardian Angel of
YOUTH

The Guardian Angel of YOUTH
AS I SHARE MY ENTHUSIASM, HUMOUR AND SENSE OF
FUN I PROTECT AND HONOUR MY YOUTHFUL SPIRIT

The Guardian Angel of Youth, whose bow and arrows and a slingshot indicate athletic prowess, is full of the vital energy and enthusiasm of the young. The energy of youth is positive and fun-loving, and this angel ensures that these qualities abound throughout the youthful stage of our lives.

ANGELIC REALM
Angel of the Heaven of Form

ANGELIC FUNCTION
To guard and protect all that is youthful in us

GIFTS FOR EARTH
It can help you to enjoy your youthful spirit;
strengthen and protect your vitality;
nourish all that is youthful about you

This angel not only guards and protects young people but also watches over everything that is youthful in all of us. It is to be expected that both people and projects are more fallible in youth. Allowances can be made for this and for curiosity and experimentation. We need a space in our lives in which we do not always have to get things right. This angel gives us the opportunity to feel it is safe to make a mistake. It helps individuals and groups discover the right way of doing things, watching over this process, protecting the vital spirit of enthusiasm at its heart.

The Guardian Angel of Youth gives our youthful spirit permission to be curious and fun-loving, exploring new avenues of growth, expression and development. It encourages creativity and leadership skills and activates youthful enthusiasm. It is this energy which helps us fulfil ourselves in later life.

This angel respects the tenderness of youth and offers respite from the heavy weight of making life decisions and of suffering the consequences if we make mistakes. The light-hearted joyfulness of spirit is what this Guardian Angel nourishes and blesses in us all.

We can offer prayers to The Guardian Angel of Youth to bless us and grant us a constant awareness of what is youthful and fun. We can ask to have our sense of excitement and enthusiasm about new projects revitalized. We can also ask this angel to bless us with the flexibility of youth, so that our spirit stays young and we are able to renew our joy in life more easily. This angel offers us the possibility of trusting in the goodness of life as well. The innocence of youth believes in the good and shares its enthusiasm for what it feels is right. The angel fosters this enthusiasm and supports our sense of fun in life.

— ✳ —

The' Guardian Angel of

YOUNG LOVE

The' Guardian Angel of YOUNG LOVE
I ACCEPT LOVE WITH GRATITUDE. I AM
OPENED AND MADE WHOLE BY ITS BEAUTY

This angel holds a pair of lovebirds. It protects the first bloom of love. It blesses our purity so that we may express the love in our hearts. It encourages us to be respectful of our bodies and be gentle with our feelings so that our first experience of love is beautiful.

ANGELIC REALM
Angel of the Heaven of Form

ANGELIC FUNCTION
To protect all who fall in love

GIFTS FOR EARTH
It can help you to value your sexuality and honour it with love;
cherish the gifts of love and an open heart;
love and respect your own tender feelings

This is the Guardian Angel who watches over young love and helps give new and tender relationships their beauty and sweetness. It is also this angel who helps us to feel safe in a relationship, and it enables us to trust in our ability to express thoughts and feelings openly and freely. This angel assists us to enhance our self-worth, and encourages intimacy with people who value us and who see our light and beauty.

We ask this angel to bless us and protect us from people who are damaging and manipulative or who are unable to share themselves in an open or honest way. We can ask this angel to support us when we feel vulnerable or insecure, and to assist us when we meet someone we would like to bond with. It can help us to take risks with someone we sense is worthwhile but who may be shy or reserved.

This Guardian Angel guides individuals towards potential partners, helping them to feel attracted to the very people who will respect their individuality and safely allow them to express their true sense of self in a kind and gentle manner. It is this angel who looks over and guides us towards making healthy friendships which will give us deep and lasting happiness.

We can pray to The Guardian Angel of Young Love whenever we enter into a relationship and need help and assurance that it is for our highest good. We can call upon this angel whenever our present relationships are stuck or stale and need revitalizing. This is the Guardian Angel who blesses and renews the spirit of love and loving sexuality within us all. We ask it to protect and guard our most intimate relationships and to keep the bonds of love secure from negative forces which may be excluding, separating or in any way attempting to place a wedge in our most cherished friendships.

— ✳ —

The Guardian Angel of

YOUNG ADULTS

The Guardian Angel of YOUNG ADULTS
I AM GUIDED AND PROTECTED AS I
BEGIN TO CHOOSE MY PATH IN LIFE

This angel carries the key which it provides for growing into happy, stable adults, able to find the balance between work and pleasure, and who know the difference between what is good and what does not serve us. It blesses us as we take responsibility for life.

ANGELIC REALM
Angel of the Heaven of Form

ANGELIC FUNCTION
To help young adults choose a clear direction

GIFTS FOR EARTH
It can help you to take responsibility for your life;
follow the direction in which your heart leads you;
make wise and careful decisions for yourself

This Guardian Angel watches over all people starting to make their own path in life. This is a time when the wholesome nurturing of childhood begins to yield results. It is also the time when we trust we are making healthy choices for our lives. This angel can help us make honest and clear decisions which can enhance our chances for growth and development. It can help guide us towards the right job choices, where our talents will be appreciated; and towards the right partners who can give us the love and encouragement we need to achieve our full potential.

This is the angel who helps us maintain a sense of humour when things appear to be going wrong or when we feel that we have lost a valuable opportunity. From this angel we can also receive assurance that we are always on the right path towards fulfilling our life's purpose. It is essential for us to recognize that no matter how many twists in the road we find on our path in life we will eventually be led to do that which allows us the opportunity to express our being to the fullest.

We can pray to our Guardian Angel to show us the right direction for our life's purpose. We can ask for comfort when we suffer loss or separation, or when we feel hurt or overwhelmed by the ways of the world and find our innate faith shaken.

This angel blesses and protects us whenever we feel we need more confidence or assurance, and comforts us when we are lonely or uncertain about how to do our very best. We can ask for trust and confidence in whatever we do, wherever we may find ourselves. With the help of this angel we can stay hopeful that everything which happens to us is for our highest good and greatest joy.

— ✶ —

The Guardian Angel of

MATURITY

The Guardian Angel of **MATURITY**
AS I TAKE RESPONSIBILITY I ALSO
DEVELOP MY STRENGTH

This angel helps us mature into wise beings capable of handling responsibilities and making fruitful choices to enhance our joy and well-being. It shows us how to age with grace. It carries the Lantern of Wisdom, and a trumpet, symbolizing an appreciation of music, one of the great beauties of life.

ANGELIC REALM
Angel of the Heaven of Form

ANGELIC FUNCTION
To guide our emotional growth

GIFTS FOR EARTH
It can help you to understand your growth process towards maturity;
allow yourself to do the things in life you have always desired;
cope with the responsibilities of adulthood

This angel helps us to make careful and wise decisions for our welfare and for the welfare of those in our care, whether we are supervisors, carers or parents.

The Guardian Angel of Maturity helps and guides us to manage high degrees of responsibility for who we are or how we want our lives to be. It helps us when we feel that the weight of our choices may be too much for us to bear and supports us in finding the right answers to the perplexing issues which confront us in our work and in our relationships.

We can pray to this angel to bless and guide us and to help us steer a course through the shoals and draughts of life's river with wisdom and insight. We can pray to be led to love and joy. We can ask that our decisions come from love and are not based on love of power. We can also ask for guidance in being mindful of the needs of younger or less responsible people entrusted to our care. This angel helps us to find the peace and wisdom which come with maturity. We may need guidance to know the difference between what simply feels good and what is truly right for us. We may ask for the courage to cultivate wisdom, and the ability to handle power so that we are not abusive. We can ask that those entrusted to our care feel safe with us. This angel can bless us with self-respect and strength of character so that the trials and difficulties of life do not become a burden, but rather enhance our essential qualities and allow us to be radiant, spiritual beings.

— ✳ —

The Guardian Angel of
HEALTH

The Guardian Angel of HEALTH
MY ATTITUDES ABOUT MYSELF ARE
RICH IN LOVE AND ACCEPTANCE

This angel, holding a basket abundantly filled with the fruits of good health, blesses us with a healthy outlook on life. It oversees the ways we look after our precious health and shows us how we can regain our stamina and positive attitudes after illness.

ANGELIC REALM
Angel of the Heaven of Form

ANGELIC FUNCTION
To guard and protect your health

GIFTS FOR EARTH
It can help you to find the energy you need to do the things you like;
look after your health better; manage your energy appropriately
so as not to exhaust yourself

This is the angel who watches over our well-being. Through the guardianship of this angel we are able to make positive decisions about the way we manage our lives. We can ask for help in leading a healthy and wholesome life-style which supports our well-being and happiness. We can ask for vitality to do all the things we love and to have abundant energy to handle all the tasks demanded of us. This angel not only supports our physical health but encourages us towards spiritual and emotional well-being. True health comes from being balanced in mind, body and spirit, and this angel can guide us towards finding this level of wholeness. It watches over us and protects us from unhealthy influences.

If we wish to improve our health by doing some exercises, eating whole and nourishing food, or having healthy breaks and holidays, then this angel is cheering us on to enjoy ourselves. We are encouraged towards a relaxing life-style, one that supports us in maintaining ease and pleasure as well as creativity and joy.

When we are ill this is the angel who watches over us and blesses our medicines and remedies with love, so as to help us heal and regain our strength and vitality. This angel is always watching out to see that we do not become ill from overdoing things.

We can offer prayers to the Guardian Angel of Health to bless us with good health and offer us healing for any physical, emotional or spiritual pains we may suffer. We ask this angel to bestow vitality and well-being upon us so that we can make the best of the tasks and projects that occupy us.

— ✳ —

The Guardian Angel of
CREATIVITY

The Guardian Angel of **CREATIVITY**
CREATIVE ENERGY FLOWS FOR ME
THE MORE I CHOOSE TO EXPRESS MY FEELINGS

This angel, carrying a tambourine and clad in finely crafted robes, helps us to channel our life force into creative acts which bring music, colour and form into our existence. It blesses us to be abundantly creative in everything we do.

ANGELIC REALM
Angel of the Heaven of Form

ANGELIC FUNCTION
To guide your creativity to flourish

GIFTS FOR EARTH
It can help you to be creative with your life;
express yourself well in everything you do;
acknowledge your creative gifts which come from the Source

This Guardian Angel watches over our creative gifts and helps us develop our self-expression. It is constantly presenting us with opportunities to expand our personal horizons. It encourages us to make the world a more beautiful and joyful place. This is the angel who stimulates our senses to see beautiful colours, devise fine designs, hear lovely music and read an abundant variety of good books.

Creativity takes endless forms and this angel inspires us to express our joy of living in a loving and caring universe. Our creativity may find its form in the way we dress, the food we cook, the way we decorate our homes or plant our gardens. It may be expressed as painting, dance, music or writing. With our angel's help we can be creative all the time. This angel offers us inspiration to change and transform the very depths of our being into those forms best suited to expressing our particular talents and imagination. It blesses all forms of our unique self-expression and wants us to share our light in whichever ways bring us pleasure and joy.

We can pray to The Guardian Angel of Creativity to guide us towards finding what is beautiful, whole, and genuine within ourselves and to allow expression to this awareness. We can ask for the grace to share our individuality with ease, and with the assurance that when we do express who we are we are confident that we are making a contribution to the well-being of everyone around us.

The more we are willing to express who we are the more we actually help make this planet a more beautiful and joyful place in which to be.

— ✶ —

The Guardian Angel of

SPIRITUAL GROWTH

The Guardian Angel of **SPIRITUAL GROWTH**
THE WAY I BECOME SPIRITUAL
IS SIMPLY TO BECOME MYSELF

This angel blesses us to live in the light of our own Divine Nature. Carrying aloft a candle with the flame of enlightenment, it points us to the lessons of life which lead to the path of the heart, enabling our spirits to be joyful and free.

ANGELIC REALM
Angel of the Heaven of Form

ANGELIC FUNCTION
To protect our growing spirituality

GIFTS FOR EARTH
It can help you to allow your spirituality to shine;
acknowledge the source of all life;
see the light in everyone around you

The primary purpose of our earthly incarnation is our development as spiritual beings. It is this Guardian Angel who guards our spiritual growth throughout life, always defending our souls. This angel blesses all the activities which nurture our spirit's welfare, which in fact means the things which are loving and respectful to ourselves. It helps us to discover what we need to recognize: the fact that we are loved and cherished. If what our spirit needs is fun then this angel will encourage us to lighten up and perhaps seek the company of a good friend and have an enjoyable time.

This angel guides us to the small pleasures which help us look after our needs and value ourselves. It encourages us to seek ways fitting our means and our outlook which enhance and nourish our being. Its guidance may be as simple as directing us to slow down and take a walk on a sunny afternoon, or have a hot bath with lots of essential oils and a candle. Our spirituality blossoms when we look after ourselves. This angel ensures that we have the opportunity to choose activities and people that will support our spirit in growing and flourishing. It blesses us with love, so that we feel the grace of our soul and allow the sun to shine in our hearts.

We can offer up prayers to The Guardian Angel of Spiritual Growth so that we are guided towards those people and books best able to nurture our spiritual development. We may ask for self-awareness to be able to tune into our own feelings. We may need stillness and peace to hear our inner voice and to know our heart's desires. We pray that those who teach spiritual truths have an open heart and are compassionate to those who seek guidance and development. We ask this angel to bless the seekers and the masters so we may realize that we are all one with the Source.

This angel teaches us the importance of faith and encourages us to retain our faith in the goodness of life, even when things are in flux and we are filled with uncertainties. It inspires us when we seek ideas and is constantly leading us to the realization that we are aspects of God's love.

The Guardian Angel of
SERVICE

The Guardian Angel of **SERVICE**
I OFFER THE BEST OF MY TALENTS AND GOODWILL,
MAKING MY PLACE IN THE UNIVERSE A BETTER ONE

This angel holds a dove, symbolizing willingness to help. It blesses all who dedicate their life energy to helping to make this planet a happier and an easier place to live in. It brings the light of Divine Grace to all who willingly give their lives to the service of helping others.

ANGELIC REALM
Angel of the Heaven of Form

ANGELIC FUNCTION
To teach us how to give from our hearts

GIFTS FOR EARTH
It can help you to understand the nature of giving to others;
allow yourself to be given to;
appreciate the spiritual function of service

This Guardian Angel looks after and blesses all those who serve; those people who have a feeling in their hearts that they would like to help make this earth a more peaceful and fruitful place for us all. For those who truly believe that what really matters is helping to get things right for the rest of us, this angel offers energy, inspiration, contacts and resources so that the jobs at hand can get done in the best possible way.

These acts of service may come under the heading of civic or government work, or may be the warm gestures of love and care from volunteers, helpers or therapists. They may include simple personal favours from people who offer help; in fact, anyone who offers humane assistance in one form or another can be said to give service.

These people are blessed by the appreciation and acknowledgement that their services make a difference in others' lives. This world would be a less lovely or workable place without the service of so many people who give their time and energy for the betterment of everyone.

We can pray to The Guardian Angel of Service to help us find the inner and outer resources to give in the best way we are able, so as to help our young and old people, to serve our churches and temples, and to engage in decision-making policy for our neighbourhoods or our governments.

Service is the way we can participate in our communities and make a real and lasting contribution to the welfare of others. We ask blessings on all those who serve in any capacity to help make this a better world for us all to live in.

The Angel Prince of
THE SOUTH

The Angel Prince of **THE SOUTH**
I LET GO OF ALL PAIN AND TENSION AS
I FLOAT IN THE SEA OF DIVINE LOVE

This angel rules over the element of earth and the psychological function of sensation. It holds a sheaf of wheat, to emphasize its association with the fruits of the earth. It inspires us to look after our planet and the needs of our physical bodies with care and awareness.

ANGELIC REALM
Angel of the Heaven of Form

HEAVENLY FUNCTION
To guide and protect the multitude of people within its realm

GIFTS FOR EARTH
It can help you to feel well in your body; awaken your senses;
earth your energy so that you are better able to manifest your
gifts and make your dreams come true

This angel gives us guidance in all aspects of 'grounding' ourselves in material reality. It blesses our senses so that we may fully experience the world around us in and through our physical bodies. We use the earth element to ground our spirituality in the world of form, and this enables us to manifest our highest hopes and realize our dreams. The shift from creative thought to physical form requires us to use all our senses to the best of our abilities. Earthing our energy gives us structure, stability and security, so that we may realize our true creative nature.

We can pray to The Angel Prince of the South to bless our senses and help us to materialize our dreams. This angel also blesses us with bodily ease, so that we are freed from stress and tension and are better able to experience pleasure. When we are well in our bodies we release good energy, which is healing to ourselves and those around us. It is how we make our planet a better place by actually being happy.

The Angel Prince of the South encourages us to listen to our bodies and to treat ourselves respectfully. This means that we look after ourselves, feeding, clothing, resting and exercising our bodies with care and thought. Under this angel's guidance we can become sensitive caretakers of the temple which houses the spirit. This angel can help us stop abusive habits which weaken the body. Our senses are most alive when we give ourselves healthy food, clothing made from natural fibre, sufficient rest and ample exercise and space to be ourselves. We honour this angel when we honour our physical form, and it, in return, blesses us. This angel encourages and supports us in our efforts to be grounded on the earth plane and in expressing and sharing ourselves.

— ✶ —

The Angel Prince of
THE NORTH

The Angel Prince of **THE NORTH**
I CELEBRATE MY UNIQUENESS
WITH JOY AND GRATITUDE

This angel rules over the element of air and the psychological function of thinking. It carries the sun of consciousness. It aids and supports all efforts towards clear and lucid thinking, and encourages us to find the balance between this over-used function and the other three functions.

ANGELIC REALM
Angel of the Heaven of Form

HEAVENLY FUNCTION
To encourage the multitudes and assist world leaders in rational thought

GIFTS FOR EARTH
It can help you to keep your thoughts positive and affirmative;
engage in clear and focused thinking;
utilize your thinking for your highest good and greatest joy

Positive thinking and understanding allow us to express our freedom and individuality. This Angel Prince helps us to communicate our ideas to others and aids us in forming a rational plan for living our lives. Clarity of thought permits us to be economical with our energy and wise with our actions.

We can pray to The Angel Prince of the North to bless us with insight and to help us focus our thinking clearly. We can also pray for help with our ability to express our thoughts, so that our ideas are made clear and are easily understood and accepted by others. This angel can help us comprehend difficult concepts. These can include new ideas which may be difficult to assimilate, or they could be concepts which are alien to our belief system. This angel helps us to keep an open mind and expand our ideas about life and the universe. It can ease the path for us in learning anything which is hard to grasp.

We ask The Angel Prince of the North to bless us with the ability to transform our negative thinking into healthy, positive thoughts which reflect high self-esteem and self-respect. We ask for positive, clear thinking which helps us look beyond a dark situation to a future which is bright and full of good things for us and for those we love.

The Angel Prince of the North can help us expand our capacity for clear thought. We can pray that it opens our brow chakra to illuminate our rational and conceptual processes. We look to be able to broaden our thinking through excellent educational and training programmes. Good libraries and uplifting books help us to develop our faculties and this angel can support us in having a fully functional mental capacity. It can aid us in our on-going intellectual growth and development. It can show us how to stay receptive to new ideas and at the same time be discerning about the options and choices we make for our lives.

— ✷ —

The Angel Prince of
THE EAST

The Angel Prince of **THE EAST**
I PURIFY MY MIND BY AFFIRMING MY WORTH
AND HONOURING MY CHOICES FOR LOVE

This angel rules over the element of water and the psychological function of feeling. It carries a chalice, holding the water of life, and hovers over the sea, which represents undifferentiated emotion. This angel helps us to express our feelings and balance our emotions.

ANGELIC REALM
Angel of the Heaven of Form

HEAVENLY FUNCTION
To help the multitudes open and express their feelings

GIFTS FOR EARTH
It can help you to accept your feelings; open your heart;
feel safe expressing yourself and your innermost feelings

Our feelings are a strong and elemental force which can unleash great waves of emotion. Feelings, if unexpressed, ferment and form an unconscious pull of their own, eventually demanding to be expressed and resolved. When we are open to feelings, on the other hand, emotions flow like water. What we seek is a balance in which we are aware of our feelings and can also express them. We want to feel what is true for us rather than suppress our life force in bottled-up emotions. Repressed anger, sadness or anxiety will inevitably draw us into situations which can act like a magnet, pulling our feelings up to the surface. If we are unaware, our emotional projections may make us feel we are the victims of a situation, rather than owning that it has been created out of our unexpressed emotions.

The Angel Prince of the East helps and guides us to experience the richness of our feelings and to find legitimate and creative outlets for them. He blesses us each time we allow our emotions honest acknowledgement, and he helps us to transmute negative feelings into legitimate creative expression. He shows us how to paint, sing, or dance our feelings so that they do not stay locked in our unconscious, fomenting situations which only lead to more pain. We can pray to this angel to help us feel comfortable with our feelings and not to get caught up in judging ourselves for whatever they may be. When we allow ourselves to feel our feelings we are connecting to the depths of our spirit.

The Angel Prince of the East offers us the support and comfort we need to experience and express our feelings. When we do this we are more fully alive, in the mainstream of life. When we allow our feelings to flow we are giving ourselves the gift of release and empowering ourselves to be more truly who we are. With each expression of sadness or anger that we own and integrate into our personality we grow and mature. True self-empowerment can happen only when we allow our feelings scope. They are, after all, part and parcel of our being, and this angel wants us to feel safe with what we feel.

The Angel Prince of

THE WEST

The Angel Prince of THE WEST
I CREATE THE REALITY AROUND ME WITH
THOUGHTS OF PURE LOVE AND GOODNESS

This angel rules over the element of fire and the psychological function of intuition. It carries a torch, signifying intuitive illumination. The fire of intuition can open the chasm between the visible and the invisible world. It allows us access to the depths of our knowing, which is locked within our cellular memory.

ANGELIC REALM
Angel of the Heaven of Form

HEAVENLY FUNCTION
To provide the multitude with access to the heavenly realms

GIFTS FOR EARTH
It can help you to understand the true nature of people and situations;
develop your intuition and trust your inner knowing;
help you experience life through other dimensions

Intuition is our capacity to know our inner truths. It is a nonrational function and comes from a very deep place within us which was probably our first level of understanding. It is a precursor of rational thinking and is more closely associated with our feeling function. Intuition is the ability to know something to be true from deep within ourselves. It is the truest, and, in some sense, the most immediate way of seeing the reality of self and others.

The Angel Prince of the West enables us to gather information which we can then use positively for our growth and development. We unconsciously use our intuition all the time as a way of knowing if something or someone is right for us or if we are safe. We can sharpen our consciousness of this function by increasing our awareness and by practice at listening to our inner voice.

The angels generally express themselves to us through pictures, which we then interpret with our rational minds. But to understand fully the guidance we are given from the higher spiritual realms we need clearly focused intuition. We need to be able consciously to read the signals filtering through our minds, so as to decode them.

We pray to The Angel Prince of the West to open our capacity for intuition and inner knowing and to help us utilize this gift. This means that we need to be willing to recognize the projections of our own emotions on to the people and world around us. Such projections often prevent us from seeing a situation with clarity. We can ask The Angel Prince of the West to help us stand out of the way of our projections, so that our inner vision is clear and pure.

Clear vision and intuition are the gifts of mystics and can be developed by anyone who values this type of knowledge, though they have not been highly esteemed in the western world until fairly recently. This angel offers us the realization of one of our innate gifts if only we choose to grasp it for ourselves.

— ✳ —

THE HEAVEN OF CREATION

The Heaven of Creation is the second level of the heavenly realms. We can connect with its highly refined energy to illuminate our personal relationships. The angels of this realm are known by their specific names of the Powers, the Virtues and the Dominions. They all help us to love and understand one another.

So many people find relationships fraught and stressful. The angels of the Heaven of Creation help to make them easier, so that we have meaning and intimacy in our lives. The angels try to teach us to cherish one another as best we can. Inside everyone is the heart of an angel. If only we can allow this to show through, we would all live happily. The angels from the Heaven of Creation provide us with the tools we need to make our relationships work. They are always trying to show us the healthy and wholesome ways which enable us to flourish as free and creative spirits.

It is in relationships that we have the opportunity to know ourselves. They help us to accept our limitations, expand our horizons and develop our strengths. They contain within them the matching mirrors of our souls. They help us to identify our self-worth, our capacity for love, pleasure and humour. They enlighten us about our integrity or where we collude with other people. Relationships test our principles about loyalty, trust and honesty. They help us refine our needs and look at our ambitions and desires. They show us the heights and depths of emotions. It is through relationships that the angels teach us about love and wisdom. They offer us the key to freedom and trust when our lives may be clouded with unhappiness. They are there to smooth the way so that our relationships can give us joy and pleasure.

The angels want us to be happy, joyful and playful. Their intent is to see us fulfilled in every way. They offer us their support and love to help us find our joy. They nourish and protect our souls so that we can live out our freedom and express our creative natures fully. They are life-enhancers, facilitating our growth in ways that teach us about the infinite power of the Source. Angels remind us that we have the freedom to make our lives as pleasurable as we want. It is then up to us to make them fulfilling and to express our gratitude for all we have been given, for there is no true healing without gratitude. The more we open our hearts to allow in peace, freedom and reconciliation, the greater our aliveness and joy.

The Powers

For an angel of peace, a faithful guide, a guardian of our souls and bodies,
let us entreat the Lord

LITURGY OF THE EASTERN ORTHODOX CHURCH

The protecting and guiding angels known as the Powers are the angels who specifically offer us peace, harmony and serenity. Their heavenly function is to guard our souls, which thrive best in an atmosphere of tranquillity and peace. When we seek a peaceful life the angels help us transform the emotional turmoil of our lives into serenity. They know that we are happier and healthier when we seek peace in ourselves and in our world. We then have the opportunity to thrive emotionally and become creative individuals. They are absolutely clear, however, that it is our free choice to want this as a way of life. They never impose on us, but allow our free choice to flourish and bloom as we evolve out of struggle and survival into whole and integrated human beings.

When we do choose peace the Powers help us release whatever is fraught and dramatic in our lives. They help us find peaceful, gentle ways for our souls to thrive and prosper so that, ultimately, we can be happy. A prayer from The Gospel of the Essenes beseeching peace says:

O Heavenly Father!
Bring unto thy earth the reign of Peace!
Then shall we remember the words
Of him who taught of old the Children of Light:
I give the peace of thy Earthly Mother
To thy body,
And the peace of thy Heavenly Father
To thy spirit.
And let the peace of both
Reign among the sons of men.
Come to me all that are weary,
And that struggle in strife and affliction!
For my peace will strengthen thee and comfort thee.
For my peace is exceedingly full of joy.

The Virtues

The Virtues teach us the love of freedom and the sanctity of faith. Their heavenly function is to transform our thoughts into matter. They are the essential link in the process we call manifestation. This means that what we wish for and desire can be transformed into material reality by our firm intention to create it. In order for some desired thing to manifest itself in our everyday existence, we need to have faith that it is possible for us to have what we want. When we accept that something can become a real possibility for us, and we let go of the idea of it and trust with all our hearts, then, if it is for our highest good and greatest joy, it will come into our lives. The Virtues help the process of manifestation along by transforming our dreams into reality. They teach us that we are free to desire whatever we feel will give us happiness and pleasure. They help our lives unfold in the ways we would like them to. They remind us how important it is to trust in the positive and be creative in our thinking.

They bring us the lessons of freedom, trust and faith. It is their guidance through tough and difficult times which sustains us. They help us value and cherish these qualities, for they know that nothing is truly possible in terms of real and lasting manifestation which does not embody them.

We are freedom itself, and yet so many of our relationships are expressions of collusion and co-dependency rather than of our more evolved and free self. As we grow, it takes trust in the process of life itself to know we are moving towards the Light and our own individuation. Faith is the most essential quality for knowing that all is possible and that we are truly protected and guided.

The Dominions

*The angels sing the praise of their Lord and ask
forgiveness for those on earth*

THE KORAN XLII:5

The Dominions offer mankind the quality of mercy. They help us to reconcile our past and find forgiveness in our hearts. They also bring us the gift of wisdom, enabling us to live in a state of grace. They help us come more fully into the present by releasing the cumbersome energy of past recriminations, which can weigh heavily on our spirits and stop our creative force.

The Dominions are angels of great light and sensitivity. They know that often, for most of us, forgiveness is one of the hardest things that can be asked of us. Where there has been great suffering, sometimes for generations, hatred and pain are ingrained in us. These divine spirits gently coax us to release the bondage of our negativity over and over again. They lovingly ease the weight of our suffering and make it possible for us to let go of the past and live more fully in the moment.

Powers: The Angel of

PEACE

The Angel of PEACE
I OPEN MY HEART AND REST IN
THE PEACE OF DIVINE LOVE

This angel signifies the blessings that peace can bring. The swirling cloak envelops it in heavenly peace. The doves in flight symbolize both the release of our primary fears and the benefits of peace to include calm and contentment.

ANGELIC REALM
Angel of the Heaven of Creation

HEAVENLY FUNCTION
To guide our souls to peace

GIFTS FOR EARTH
It can help us to reconcile opposite forces in our lives;
find solutions to conflicts and paradoxes;
teach us how to be at peace with ourselves

The Angel of Peace channels the energy we need to resolve conflicts and paradoxes in our lives. It helps us to live a life compatible with our needs and desires, giving us the opportunity to flourish in a peaceful way. This angel smooths the path to peace so that we can find love and accept ourselves. Peace offers us the possibility of living in a way that is congruent with our natural rhythms and cycles and that honours our potential gifts and abilities.

Once we have released our primary fears about basic survival we start to learn to trust in the goodness of life. Many of us may reach this level of development as we mature and after we have weathered crisis, pain or loss, only to find that we are fine and deeply intact at our core. At our very centre we are pure peace, and this cannot be destroyed or diminished by external circumstances. We can choose to identify with this part of ourselves when we open our hearts to The Angel of Peace.

Once we have resolved the conflicts within ourselves, our lives begin to take on a deeper sense of peace and order which lets us flourish as the unique and creative beings we are. It is only when we are at peace that we can truly be creative. Otherwise we are limited to continually re-enacting the painful traumas of our lives.

We can offer prayers to The Angel of Peace to bring peace to our planet, peace to our families and friends and, most importantly, peace to ourselves so that we may resolve the dilemmas and paradoxes we face. This way we can finally come to rest in the certainty that we are a vital part of creation and have a worthwhile and meaningful part to play.

We can appeal to this angel for peace of mind, heart and soul as we become internally stiller and less reactive to external conflict around us. This angel will guide us towards healthy situations and to people who will allow us to live in peace. This peace is lasting and sustaining and we can draw upon its strength whenever we need it. The Angel of Peace offers us its gifts every time we are stressed and tense. It will wrap you in a cloak of comfort to let you be at peace with yourself.

Powers: The Angel of
SERENITY

The Angel of **SERENITY**
I FEEL SERENE AND TRANQUIL
WHEN I ACCEPT WHO I AM

The Angel of Serenity is carrying the dove that symbolizes the serenity of life. The calm stance evokes the tranquillity and peace that are this angel's gift to us. Serenity is a blessing that enables us to feel safe and comfortable. With the gift of serenity we have the opportunity to be fruitful in our lives.

ANGELIC REALM
Angel of the Heaven of Creation

HEAVENLY FUNCTION
To let our souls be serene

GIFTS FOR EARTH
It can help us to live our lives serenely;
find solutions to conflicts;
find ultimate happiness with ourselves

The Angel of Serenity dances with us as we engage in daily struggles and conflicts. This angel wishes us the ease of serenity, and will often stimulate our dreams to create a vision of how life could be if only we dared to live from that place within ourselves. This angel will always encourage us to disengage from struggle and conflict. This is done by changing our attitude and reframing our view of a situation or person.

The gift of serenity comes when we have surrendered our struggles and given up our negativity. It is a gift that may be shaken from time to time, but once we have had the experience of it we will always want it in our lives. We may partake of spiritual and esoteric practice to try to achieve this state. In truth, serenity, like peace, is always there for us when we slow our lives down to a pace where we can feel our feelings and tune into the oneness of the Source. We can offer prayers to this angel to give us a taste of serenity so that we can make the adjustments and changes necessary to live from our inner being.

Serenity means giving up the struggle and releasing the ego to live in a truly congruent way with our Higher Self. We can pray to attain this spiritual state, which means knowing that the universe is a benign and safe place and that we truly belong here. When we accept our oneness with the Source we can be serene through crisis, change and loss. This quality comes with a spiritual attitude which recognizes that everything is as it should be and that we are in the right place, doing the right thing. This means giving up attitudes which stand in the way of being happy. It also means releasing emotional pain which can lead us to believe that life has to be tortuous or fraught.

Praying to The Angel of Serenity opens the channel for this essence of God's love to permeate our lives. It allows us to live from a deep and rich centre, unshaken by difficult circumstances. We pray for help to eliminate the obstacles to serenity which clutter our lives. We can also ask the angel to help us feel that we deserve to live in a serene way so that our purpose can be fulfilled with ease and grace.

Powers: The Angel of

HARMONY

The Angel of HARMONY
I LIVE IN HARMONY WHEN I AM
AT ONE WITH THE SOURCE

The Angel of Harmony is attended by the most beautiful birds of the air, flocking to the sanctuary of its peaceful spirit. Symbols of flourishing concord, the songbirds show the sense of harmony that good relationships can give to us.

ANGELIC REALM
Angel of the Heaven of Creation

ANGELIC FUNCTION
To let our souls rest in harmony

GIFTS FOR EARTH
It can help us to live a harmonious life;
seek out people and places which are harmonious;
help us to express our spirits in a harmonious way

The Angel of Harmony shares its grace with us when we choose to live a harmonious life. Living in harmony entails many things. It has a physical aspect, which can be found in the environment we choose to live in. It is also an emotional state, reflecting the degrees of openness, honesty and integrity we bring into our lives. We live in harmony, in part, when we accept our dependence on the earth which nourishes us and supports life. We are in harmony with our feelings when we give them the space to be real for us.

Living in harmony with ourselves means we honour our own special gifts. When we live in harmony with universal truth we seek to give of our best and to receive with an open heart. Living in harmony is an actual energy state, from which we may experience life in an optimal state of flow. This means that we want good, wholesome food to enrich our bodies, and we avoid all forms of substance abuse. We need to have enough rest and recreation on a regular basis and to do work that is both creative and emotionally satisfying. Play, rest, good friends, beauty and spiritual stimulation are all vital ingredients in a truly harmonious life.

To live in harmony with our deep inner nature is to live in accordance with universal truths. These truths exist in all religions and are accepted among all cultures throughout the ages. They are the basis of an ethical code which respects the dignity of the individual.

We live in harmony when we release the past and process out our negativity. Holding on to negative energy is the basis for disharmony and is known as disease. Lastly, we find gratitude in our hearts for all the good things we have been given. Gratitude will always give us the sense that we are living in harmony.

We can appeal to The Angel of Harmony to help us find the right path to harmony, and can ask for assistance in honouring whatever we may require to make our lives more joyful and creative. Harmony is a balance between the spiritual, emotional and physical planes.

Virtues: The Angel of

FREEDOM

The Angel of **FREEDOM**
I AM ALWAYS FREE TO CHOOSE LOVE,
INDEPENDENCE AND CREATIVITY

The Angel of Freedom is shown with a beautiful stole flying freely in the wind, a symbol of the flow of life energy. This angel guards the spirit's right to express independence and creativity as it watches over the world, protecting our freedom.

ANGELIC REALM
Angel of the Heaven of Creation

ANGELIC FUNCTION
To remove the obstacles to freedom

GIFTS FOR EARTH
It can help us to find our freedom;
value its place in our lives;
cherish it in our relationships of all kinds

The Angel of Freedom blesses us and helps us realize the freedom of the divine spirit within us. It offers untold gifts when we allow freedom to be an integral part of our lives. We need only to desire the experience of our freedom and this angel will assist us in knowing it at every turn. It will help us realize that freedom is who we are.

There are many aspects to freedom, and this angel will show us the numerous ways in which we can share in its gift. It may mean freedom from the constraints of our worldly existence. It could as well mean a deep experience of who we are at core, and that is an awareness rather than something we do. It is not freedom from something as much as freedom to be ourselves which this angel brings to our consciousness.

We can pray to The Angel of Freedom to open our hearts and our minds to the meaning of freedom. And we may find that, as a result, we need to look at our ability to communicate our needs or speak up for ourselves in order to facilitate our leap into freedom.

Sometimes we are thrown the gift of freedom before we are consciously ready for it, and then we take a while to integrate our experience and to let go of our old patterns which tie us to preconceived ideas about how life should be. We are always free to choose how we want to go through life: tied to old ideas, or open to the unlimited opportunities to express ourselves. The more freedom we allow ourselves the more joyful and unlimited our scope for expression. We offer prayers to The Angel of Freedom to remove the obstacles which limit our self-expression, health and joy. We ask that we may have the capacity to nurture freedom rather than abuse it in a self-destructive way. We ask that people everywhere be permitted to choose the gift of freedom.

This angel works in subtle ways to encourage us. It sends us Light and courage to satisfy our yearning for freedom. It is never far from us as we pursue our path to growth and development. It helps us assimilate this awareness from the depths of our souls as free spirits, worthy of the opportunity to express ourselves.

Virtues: The Angel of

TRUST

The Angel of **TRUST**
I TRUST IN THE DIVINE POWER OF GOODNESS
AND LOVE TO PROTECT AND GUIDE ME

The Angel of Trust is represented holding the stole, which it uses as a blindfold. When we are blindfolded we have to trust in ourselves and in God, knowing that we are protected by this guardian angel, whose hands reach out to us across the gulf of time and worldly matters to offer goodness freely.

ANGELIC REALM
Angel of the Heaven of Creation

ANGELIC FUNCTION
To open our hearts and minds to trusting in the goodness of life

GIFTS FOR EARTH
It can help us to learn to trust ourselves;
learn to trust in life itself and all it has to offer us;
learn to trust other people

The Angel of Trust works with our Higher Self to help us express and develop a trusting attitude towards life. This trust can manifest itself when we are caught on the fence, torn between being negative, cynical or destructive and wishing to be positive and believe that our highest good and greatest joy are being fulfilled.

This angel offers us the essential love of spirit we need in order to trust and be truly life-affirming. Trust can make all the difference in the qualitative experiences of our life. To be able to trust is an essential ingredient of happiness and ease, otherwise our energy will be tied up with suspicion, doubt and fear. Trust gives us the courage to move forward or take risks that we would not be able to take if we lacked this one component vital to growth and spirituality.

The Angel of Trust helps each one of us to value our experiences and trust our perceptions. Only through listening to our inner wisdom can we develop the quality of trust which we so vitally need in order to progress through life. When we learn to trust in the goodness of life we have a more joyful time and more worthwhile contacts with others.

Odd though it may sound, trust reflects itself in all our choices, from the relationships we form, to the jobs and careers we pick, right through to the type of clothes we wear. When we are lacking in trust we will always be carrying an umbrella and choosing the safest, least challenging way of doing something, fearful of hurt or of doing it wrong. It is only when we dare to take risks, to stand up for what we feel and to trust in our inner sense of right and wrong that we eventually develop a sense of mastery about life.

We can offer prayers to this angel to help us trust our inner sense of knowing. We can ask for trust in one another so that we can feel safe expressing our love and care for one another. This angel wants our life experiences to be healthy and nourishing. Nothing is more undermining to our spirits than cunning or betrayal.

— ✶ —

Virtues: The Angel of

FAITH

The Angel of FAITH
I HAVE FAITH THAT GOODNESS AND
JOY ARE MINE, NOW AND FOREVER

The Angel of Faith stands serene in the knowledge that faith is abiding. It holds the sacred stole which wraps us in a deep faith, and which symbolizes its protection through the troubles of life. It reminds us what is asked of us when we keep our faith.

ANGELIC REALM
Angel of the Heaven of Creation

ANGELIC FUNCTION
To help mankind find faith in God and His angels

GIFTS FOR EARTH
It can help us to have faith when things are difficult;
express our faith in the goodness of life;
let faith be our guiding light throughout our lives

We may find, when life's trials are weighing heavily on us, that we can find the faith that all will come right. This faith sustains us through the hard times. We may sometimes stumble along and lose our way, but faith that all is ultimately for our highest good can raise us above our doubts and despair. Faith is the belief that whatever it is you are asking God to deliver is already on its way. Faith is the acceptance of uncertainty and the firm belief that all comes right in the end.

In this age of instant gratification we lack the opportunities to express our faith except when grave crisis comes along. Faith is something that only we can choose to develop for ourselves; no one can give it to us or even tell us how to cultivate it. People can tell us about it and recount their own personal experiences but essentially it comes to each of us from a deep inner connection with ourselves.

Life is really very simple when we have faith. We can follow our heart and live a committed and meaningful life in the faith that we are fulfilling a plan. We rise above our limited egos to have faith in the knowledge that this is a benign and loving universe and that we are a part of the catalyst which is changing the world to a better place.

Faith helps us to wait in patience for the light when we can see only the darkness in front of us. It is an essential component for life to have faith that whatever our destiny is, it is right for us. Faith is an ever-deepening knowledge that we are guided, loved and protected at all times. We need only surrender to that love to let the purpose of our lives be fulfilled.

We can pray to The Angel of Faith to help us renew our faith in the process of life. It will help us to accept those things which we cannot change, as well as all that has been given us to work with and refine in our lives. Ultimately, it will carry us through rough and difficult transitions and help us to renew our love for Self and humanity. The Angel of Faith is there to help us bridge the gap between this material, worldly life and the spiritual plane.

Dominions: The Angel of

RECONCILIATION

The Angel of RECONCILIATION
LET ME BE FULLY RECONCILED WITH
WHAT I HAVE LEFT BEHIND

This angel is shown holding a lily, which is here a symbol of reconciliation, offering hope and solace to those in need. The angel offers us the peace and wisdom we need for reconciliation. It brings the new dawn of awareness, when we start our lives afresh, living magically in the present moment.

ANGELIC REALM
Angel of the Heaven of Creation

ANGELIC FUNCTION
To reconcile us to the Light

GIFTS FOR EARTH
It can help us to release painful traumas which distort our view of life; bring us more fully into the present flow of life; help us to open our hearts to the good

The Angel of Reconciliation offers us the opportunity to clear out the old and useless baggage of our past. By becoming reconciled with the past we release the sorrows, hurts and resentments which clog and congest our energy and burden us. We need our vitality to live in the present, not to submerge our life in old grudges.

The Angel of Reconciliation works to help us integrate our past with our present reality. It helps us see spiritual truths, so that we can learn from our past. This way anything painful in our lives can be seen anew as a positive step for growth – even the most brutal experiences.

This angel is always easing the transition from the past into the present, offering us every opportunity to accept things as they are. Whether it was something which we did to others or to ourselves or whether it was something which happened to us, this angel will help us reconcile our pasts. The process of letting go of the past helps us to redeem our spirit. It releases the energy we have invested in projecting our feelings on to past situations, people and events. When we are   limited by sorrow, bereavement, grievances or bitterness we are actually destroying the vitality and enjoyment of the ever-present now. The past is a stepping-stone to wholeness if we choose to see it that way.

We can offer our prayers to The Angel of Reconciliation to help us accept the past as it was, and release our negative ideas about how it should have been. We can ask that the lessons of past experiences help us develop as healthy-minded adults who can step forward into the joy of the present. This will give us both pleasure and wisdom.

We ask this angel to show us how to integrate our past into a living present, full of joy and fulfilment. We ask for guidance in letting go of the past and accepting that we can always make a fresh start. Reconciliation is not about changing something which cannot be altered. Rather it is about transforming our view of how the past was, and how we can enhance and empower ourselves now by making positive choices for well-being.

Dominions: The Angel of

MERCY

The Angel of **MERCY**
DIVINE MERCY GIVES ME THE GRACE
TO BE TENDER AND ACCEPTING

This angel is depicted in rich robes, which enfold us in the blessing of mercy when we are weak. It brings hope and succour for those who are struggling, and renews our belief in God's all-embracing mercy. The lily is a universal symbol of purity and truth.

ANGELIC REALM
Angel of the Heaven of Creation

ANGELIC FUNCTION
To bring mercy into our lives

GIFTS FOR EARTH
It can help us to understand God's love for mankind;
make us conscious that we are protected and guided;
contemplate gratitude for the blessings in our lives

The Angel of Mercy offers us the love of God as a living reality. When we are faced with an unbearable situation and suddenly there is a shift of energy or a change in circumstances, we are being blessed by The Angel of Mercy. We are helped constantly to turn our thoughts and attitudes around through the aid of Divine mercy.

It may be in small and subtle ways that we experience mercy. It can come in the form of a friendly phone call when we are feeling despair, or a gentle boost to our confidence in circumstances where we are unsure of ourselves. It could unfold in so many situations which we do not control, or where we are affected by our conscious minds. For instance, we could meet a person who changes our lives, or we could be accepted or rejected for a job or a course of study. On reflection we begin to realize the amazing consequences that this turning point had on our lives. This may be called mere coincidence in the rational world. I, however, prefer to accept it as the gift of The Angel of Mercy, who is working to make our lives fulfilled.

What this awareness of guidance and intervention brings us is an understanding of non-doing. This means we do not have to strive and push ourselves or be harsh or punishing to ourselves because things do not work out as we wanted. Trusting in Divine Mercy as a gift from the angels enables us to participate fully in the process of our lives.

We can pray for The Angel of Mercy to be active in our lives. Without trying to control our circumstances we can accept that mercy is constantly being given us and that we can surrender to the Source. We can accept the gift of mercy by being tender and gentle with ourselves and others. When we are oblivious to mercy we are domineering and controlling, stepping on many toes, living from our ego and opening ourselves to high levels of strife. The path of acceptance offers us mercy as a gift of unconditional love. Mercy moves us through the rough patches of our lives and on to new levels of awareness where we are living more fully in the light of Divine love.

Dominions: The Angel of

FORGIVENESS

The Angel of FORGIVENESS
I CHOOSE TO FORGIVE ALL THOSE
WHO HAVE HURT ME IN THE PAST

This angel is seen holding the lily of purity with which it blesses those asking for forgiveness. Brotherhood is a natural consequence when we forgive others. Forgiveness means we release the tears of past hurts and the anger of past resentment, to live with the love of the angels in the here and now.

ANGELIC REALM
Angel of the Heaven of Creation

ANGELIC FUNCTION
To help us forgive and release the past

GIFTS FOR EARTH
It can help us to honour and empower ourselves when
we forgive others; live in the present when we forgive the past;
create the space for intimacy to thrive when we forgive others

The Angel of Forgiveness encourages and prompts us to look at past hurts and resentments in a new light. We gain in self-respect and wisdom when we are able to let go of the past and forgive those who have hurt us. Otherwise we remain stuck in believing we are victims, with no possibility of altering our lives.

Forgiveness does not mean we condone bad behaviour, nor does it mean we necessarily have to like the people who treated us badly. It does mean, however, that as we forgive others we release our anger and resentment. When we forgive we are left with lightness of spirit and a good feeling about ourselves. Without that we do not have any possibility for true empowerment. We would still believe that others did us wrong and we would always carry that resentment. It corrodes our insides; it is the stuff disease is made of. We perpetrate abuse and in-justice on ourselves by carrying negative feelings around with us.

Forgiveness sets us free and helps to open up a deeper channel for relating to others. We may need help to forgive, and The Angel of Forgiveness offers us the grace to find tenderness in our hearts and the courage to ask for assistance when forgiveness seems too daunting a task. Forgiveness helps us to be receptive to healing and to love. When we forgive we are increasing our levels of self-esteem, because, in fact, the point of real power rests only within us. We are, in effect, saying we no longer wish to be victims of abuse, treachery, or any other form of negativity which impedes our happiness. Forgiveness, like acknowledgement, is what helps us grow into happy and healthy people.

We can ask The Angel of Forgiveness to show us the path to releasing blame and hurt. It is really only our willingness to free ourselves from the burden of negativity that will kick-start the process of healing. This release gives us the opportunity to clean up other aspects of our lives where there may be hidden resentments and sorrows blocking our joy. By asking The Angel of Forgiveness to help us release our negativity we are enabling the process of healing to start.

THE HEAVEN OF PARADISE

We come to the level of Heaven which is the closest to the Divine Presence. This is where we surrender our ego to the unconditional love of God and His angels. Our souls are at one here, attuned to Divine wisdom and love. It is within this realm that we live from the reality of our hearts, where there is no separation between our will and God's will. At this level we are beyond conflict, separation and doubt.

The Heaven of Paradise is the realm of bliss and pure joy. It is where creation happens effortlessly and where our human experiences are harmonious and complete. There is no turmoil or need for survival here, because the spirit has transcended earthly struggles.

In the Heaven of Form the angels offered us the help we needed to manage our lives on the physical plane. On that first level we averted disaster, overcame perils and renounced negativity. The Archangels showed us the way towards healing and the evolutionary path towards wholeness of being. Our Guardian Angels guided us through the cycles of maturity and growth.

We then directed our energies to our relationships, allowing our spirits to be strengthened through purifying our thoughts and attitudes and releasing our blocked and negative feelings. We now come to that place within the heavenly spheres where love and wisdom reign and we are gently and tenderly guided towards connecting with the Source which lives within us. The closer we come to the Source the more we become aware that it is not separate from us – we are, in fact, one with it.

We come to experience the total Oneness of the Source in all things. We are not merely witness to the creation but rather an intrinsic part of the glory that expresses that Unity and Oneness.

It is in this Heaven that our dreams materialize, for this is the realm of miracles. Here creativity is perpetually manifesting the power and glory of the Divine. The angels of this Heaven offer us the greatest gifts of love and wisdom. When we open our hearts we are flooded with the joy of God's love for us and attune ourselves to be co-creators with the Source. At this level we work together with the angels.

The three types of angel in the Heaven of Paradise are the Seraphim, the Cherubim, and the Ophanim, better known as the Thrones because they sit closest to the Throne of the Divine.

The Seraphim

The Angels who are the Makers and Governors,
The Shapers and Overseers,
The Keepers and Preservers of the abundant Earth!
And of all Creations of the Heavenly Father.
We invoke the good, the strong, the beneficent
Angels of the Heavenly Father and the Earthly Mother!
That of the Light!
That of the Sky!
That of the Waters!
That of the Plants!
That of the Children of Light!
That of the Eternal Holy Creation!
We worship the Angels
Who first listened unto the thought and teaching
Of the Heavenly Father,
Of whom the Angels formed the seed of the nations.

THE GOSPEL OF THE ESSENES

The Seraphim are associated with the very essence of creation. They, in their light, are the creators of miracles. They transmit God's energy to create the elemental substance of which life is formed, and which is pervasive throughout the universe. They are known as the Angels of the Miracle of Love. They eternally offer each of us un- conditional love. They encourage and support our spiritual evolution to the highest degree, until we are at one with the creative spirit of the Source.

In THE ANGEL ORACLE they are called The Angel of the Miracle of Love, The Angel of the Essence of Love, and The Angel of Eternal Love. They represent the spirit of magnificence which we know as unconditional and eternally abiding love. We are witness to it in each act of creation. It inundates the universe with its very power. It is through the Seraphim that we come to connect with and acknowledge the splendour of this love.

The Seraphim offer, to each of us who seeks this blissful state of one-ness with the Source, ways of refining and tuning our vibrations to the highest levels of awareness. They may, for instance, bring us the miracle of unique teachers or masters, who may be non-physical as well as physical beings. These teachers are themselves beings who have come in contact with the Light and have through various means of purification burned away the dross of their negativity, surrendering to the oneness of life.

The Seraphim constantly remind us of the miracle of love, and of how we are renewed and made whole by this wondrous energy. They help us to heal the pain of all separation and loss, to realize that love is eternal and is absolutely indivisible.

The Cherubim

The Cherubim guard the entrance to Paradise. They are the bearers of the ultimate wisdom within the universe. They aid all who are associated with wisdom and they offer strength to all who are attuned to the word of God. They fill the universe with God's wisdom. When we are attuned to the vibration of their love we experience the depths of knowing within ourselves. This is a direct and clear reflection of the wisdom they channel to us, in the hope that we will know God and realize the magnitude of the unconditional love that lives within us.

The Cherubim offer us their crystal-clear awareness about the unity of all life. In the Oracle they are known as The Angel of Wisdom, The Angel of Discernment and The Angel of Knowing. They are God's messengers, who share the fullness of love and knowledge. They offer us the possibility of knowing the mysteries of life through the transmuting of knowledge into wisdom. They are not the chubby little children that are so often depicted in angelic art, but rather they are the purity of spirit that is embodied in young children who know they are safe and deeply loved.

The Thrones

The Thrones are the closest angelic form to the Divine Source itself. They exist beyond form and yet their angelic function is to transform thoughts into matter. They exist at the level of pure thought and are the conductors of the vibration of God's love into material form.

They act as the Eyes of God and take the form of swirling streams of coloured light. In the Oracle they are known as The Angel of Being, The Angel of Power and The Angel of Glory. They transmit the power and glory of the Source throughout the universe, offering a constant beam of light to enable us to manifest this love in our lives. When we release our minds and are openly experiencing the moment we are living the glory and splendour of creation as it was intended. It is then that the Thrones transport us into the realms of bliss.

They exist in the ever-present moment, and as we progress beyond our superficial identification – who we think we are – and start to live as co-creators of the universe together with the Source, we find we exist more completely in the present. In this way we are drawn into the realms of creativity, love and wisdom, which are so profound that we may be unable to give meaningful descriptions of our experiences. This is the Heaven of Paradise, which the poets and mystics have spoken of through the ages. All it requires of us is that we drop our egos and live openly and trustingly in the ever-present moment, free of the delusions which disempower and stunt our spirits. With the help of the angels we are all capable of living as we were meant to, in joy, in bliss and with the knowledge that we are truly loved and cherished.

The realm of the Thrones is the highest level the angels can ascend to. They give 'unending praise and thanksgiving' to the Source, knowing that this love and mercy will endure through eternity.

Seraphim: The Angel of

THE MIRACLE OF LOVE

The Angel of **THE MIRACLE OF LOVE**
I AM BROUGHT ALIVE BY THE
MIRACLE OF LOVE

The Angel is seen alongside lovebirds, a symbol of the miracle of love. The winged wheels of fire are symbolic of the Seraphim themselves. The eye at the top represents the symbol for the Heaven of Paradise. The heart at the bottom and the open hands stand for the longing for real love which all of us share.

ANGELIC REALM
Angel of the Heaven of Paradise

ANGELIC FUNCTION
To bring miracles into our lives

GIFTS FOR EARTH
It can help you to open yourself to receiving the love you desire;
cherish the love you have in your life;
acknowledge the miracle of love from the Source

82

The Angel of the Miracle of Love offers each of us the possibility of knowing God's love in a deeply meaningful and intimate way. For one it may be through parenthood, for another it may be in a spiritual or therapeutic community of brothers and sisters, for yet others it may come through a deeply personal relationship. We are each given the possibility of the miracle of love, and as unique individuals we will be offered the gift of God's love in unique ways that are perfect for us.

Our choice is to open our hearts so that we may be receptive to that love. When we choose love in our lives the angels embrace us and fill our hearts with the grace of Divine love. This miracle of love is best expressed through human interactions; for love that is holy offers its most beautiful reflection in our relationships with one another.

We can offer up our prayers to The Angel of the Miracle of Love to bless us with this most precious gift in our life. We can be receptive and clean of negativity so that our capacity to cherish and preserve this love and let it grow is constantly expanding. Love is so precious; it is our greatest treasure. In whatever form it comes we can cherish it, mindful not to take it for granted or treat it abusively. The clearer we are in ourselves, the less we will sully or expose this gift to the wrong energy. Love is so special that we can only honour and thank the Source for the experience of it. As we stay clean, working on ourselves, taking responsibility for our projections and maintaining a positive attitude, we become more and more capable of receiving God's love.

Miracles are given freely by the Holy Spirit. They are available to everyone. The only thing which is asked of us is to be ready to receive them. We are asked to purify our hearts and open our spirits to receive the gift of the miracle of love. We can pray to The Angel of the Miracle of Love to be our guide as we become aware that this is what we truly long for in our lives. To know the love within us is also to know the love which is around us. God's love has no limitations or boundaries. It permeates all living substance and can be experienced in everything.

Seraphim: *The Angel of*

THE ESSENCE OF LOVE

The Angel of THE ESSENCE OF LOVE
LET LOVE BE THE CENTRE
OF MY LIFE

The eye, the symbol for the Heaven of Paradise, casts radiant beams throughout the universe. The lion symbolizes the fire and passion that love can stir in us. This passion is seen throughout creation, which is here symbolized by the moon and stars. The fiery, winged wheels are the symbol of the Seraphim.

ANGELIC REALM
Angel of the Heaven of Paradise

ANGELIC FUNCTION
Protecting the essence of love

GIFTS FOR EARTH
It can help you to realize that at your core you are love;
experience love in all things;
share the essence of your being with others

The Angel of the Essence of Love helps us to strip off the mask of illusion and see that love is the essence of all life. This angel works to help us unfold from the limited cocoon of our ego and be the magnificent creatures of light we are. When we have penetrated the illusions of personality and the destructive nature of negativity we realize that what we are, at our core, is a fountain of love.

This love lives at the centre of every living cell in our bodies, and in the heart of all living things. The consciousness of which we are made permeates all other living substance too. Our own sweet essence is the same as the universal essence of love which unites us and bonds us intimately with the Source.

We can offer prayers to The Angel of the Essence of Love to help us recognize the essence which lies at the heart of our being. When we choose to identify with this essence we are coming from our Higher Self, which is an aspect of the Divine, rather than from that other self of the small, individual ego. We seek assistance to help us detach ourselves from the illusions of our being and to find the undying reality that we are one with the Source and with all life. We pray to be able to connect with that oneness and remember the eternal and unconditional nature of that love.

As we open our hearts to the love within us, we find that the essence of love is the basic and fundamental substance of life. Without it nothing could grow or flourish, and life would cease to exist. The Angel of the Essence of Love carefully guards this substance within each of us. When we choose to live from this space we are given untold treasures in the shape of experiences which acknowledge to us that love is who we are.

— ✳ —

Seraphim: The Angel of
ETERNAL LOVE

The Angel of **ETERNAL LOVE**
AS I LET LOVE IN IT STAYS IN
MY SOUL FOREVER

The all-seeing eye confirms that this is an angel of the Heaven of Paradise. The dolphin stands for the consciousness and joy of eternal love, as do the waves beneath it. The fiery wheels are the symbol of the Seraphim. The snake eating its tail is the oroborus, symbol for wholeness and eternity.

ANGELIC REALM
Angel of the Heaven of Paradise

ANGELIC FUNCTION
To transmit God's eternal and unconditional love

GIFTS FOR EARTH
It can help you to remember that love is forever;
release the fear that love is limited;
open to the spirit which is the Source of this love

The Angel of Eternal Love is a source of comfort and solace for anyone who grieves for lost love. In point of fact, love cannot be lost. It is indelible and remains a part of us through eternity. It is as though love becomes grafted on to our souls, and with each experience of love our soul expands and develops. It enhances and enlarges our perspective of ourselves, it helps us to realize that the universe is a safe and sweet place, meant to give us happiness and joy.

All love can be re-experienced in the conscious memory with the use of meditation, or various healing techniques. Love does not die with the physical body. It is eternal. It can be recalled when we have need of it.

The Angel of Eternal Love offers each of us who love the joy of knowing that the spirit holds the memory of love. When we have lost someone close to us the love shared does not diminish. It actually stays with us, becomes a part of us and furthers our spiritual development. This angel helps us to be aware of that fact and helps us to keep love alive in our hearts. At some point in our lives we will need its love and assistance, for we cannot escape loss in this physical world. This angel brings us comfort and the awareness that love never dies. Love can connect people through lifetimes and may even re-unite people who have loved in the past and who come together in this lifetime to complete that love. Some love can endure through ages of separation. When people are soul-mates they will find one another again, be it on this physical plane or at another, more ethereal level.

We can pray to The Angel of Eternal Love to remove the veil of unconsciousness that stands between us and our awareness of eternal love. If we are lonely or bereft we can pray to this angel to find comfort in the memory of a love which was essential for us at some time in our life. We can consciously choose to remember the love of friends, family, teachers, in fact anyone with whom we shared love. That memory stays with us and is a part of who we are. That love is indelible.

Cherubim: The Angel of

WISDOM

The Angel of **WISDOM**
WISDOM COMES FROM THE
DEPTHS OF MY EXPERIENCE

This angel is seen guarding the gates of Paradise, with the symbolic eye radiating its all-knowing beams. The angel prevents all from entering who do not know their own Divine nature. The candle signifies the flame of Wisdom, without which we are unable to experience the joys of Paradise.

ANGELIC REALM
Angel of the Heaven of Paradise

ANGELIC FUNCTION
To bring wisdom into the lives of us all

GIFTS FOR EARTH
It can help you to become receptive to the wisdom of God;
find wisdom in your life;
seek wisdom in all your experiences

This angel is the bearer of God's wisdom, which is carried throughout the universe to all those who seek to know The Word of God. This angel helps us find our wisdom by opening ourselves to the depths of our experience and knowing what is true for us.

When we give ourselves the opportunity to reflect, synthesize and distil our personal experiences we find wisdom. With it we can progress along our path, enriching our understanding and deepening our spirituality.

We are really only now beginning to see the wisdom in ancient teachings and re-apply it to our health and life-styles. Wisdom is an internal awareness which is projected on to the world around us so that we can live in peace and harmony.

The Angel of Wisdom brings us the gift of wisdom. It says in the Bible that wisdom is more valuable than gold. Certainly we need wisdom for our growth and spiritual development. Without wisdom we are at the mercy of the effects of the material world, and can easily lose our integrity and personal identity.

Wisdom is something all cultures have honoured and acknowledged. Ancient civilizations respected and revered those who through their experience had come to understand the inner meaning of life and were able to make sense of loss, trauma and separation. This quality of wisdom is something we are beginning to re-evaluate in our modern world and, it is to be hoped, respect. We can seek the help of The Angel of Wisdom to guide us to the wisdom within ourselves. It is from this place that we can make healthy and wise choices for our well-being and happiness.

We can offer our prayers to The Angel of Wisdom to show us how to make sense of the experiences of our life and how to find the meaning for ourselves. We can ask for wisdom for our healing and for the healing of our planet. It is surely through the gift of wisdom that we are able to find our bliss in life. The Angel of Wisdom is there to help us all find the wise and healing path.

Cherubim: *The Angel of*
DISCERNMENT

The Angel of DISCERNMENT
THROUGH THE GRACE OF THE DIVINE
I AM ABLE TO KNOW THE RIGHT PATH

*The Angel of Discernment
has risen above the clouds of
confusion, and holds an orb
which is expressive of clear
intention. The angel's gift is
the light of discernment, and
when we focus on this light
we are able to see what is for
our highest good. The eye is
the symbol of the Heaven
of Paradise.*

ANGELIC REALM
Angel of the Heaven of Paradise

ANGELIC FUNCTION
To offer discernment to all who walk the path of Light

GIFTS FOR EARTH
It can help you to know your right path;
choose what is really good for you;
know what will serve your highest good and greatest joy

The Angel of Discernment teaches us to honour our inner voice and to listen to our hearts. If we are given complex choices which involve making difficult decisions affecting our spiritual evolution, this angel helps us to choose the right path. It is always guiding us towards what will serve our growth and help us develop our strengths and gifts. Discernment eliminates what is negative, ineffectual and maybe potentially damaging to us. Learning discernment is refining our skill at sensing what is the healthiest and most joyful path for us.

Discernment is the ability to know what is ultimately for our greatest good. It is not necessarily the easy or the popular path. It is, however, the path best suited for our good. We can know what is right for us when we listen to our hearts and reflect on our choices. The Angel of Discernment is there to help guide our way in making the wisest choices.

Discernment is that ability to know in your head and heart that something or someone is right for you. Many people struggle to try to make a situation or a person right rather than asking if that person or situation is the best for themselves. When we are discerning we value ourselves at every level, and make choices which reflect that level of self-worth. The Angel of Discernment helps us to see things clearly and to expand our vision beyond our fears and doubts about ourselves. It helps us know what we may be afraid to see and allows us the possibility of making intelligent and heart-felt choices.

We can pray to The Angel of Discernment to help us develop our ability to listen to our inner voice. This will help us hear the angels whispering to us, and know the right choices to make. When we have learned discernment then the angels help us open fully to the treasures of our inner knowing. They never risk exposing that deep inner knowing to rejection. Discernment protects our deepest sensitivities. The angels want us to make only the best decisions for ourselves.

Cherubim: The Angel of

KNOWING

The Angel of KNOWING
MY SENSE OF INNER KNOWING
LEADS ME TO THE LIGHT

This angel is shown with the symbols of awareness and joy. Stardust is sprinkled down from heaven, the energy of love. It is the source of inspiration, when our desires and wishes can be made reality. The angel holds the ring of knowledge, from which all our awareness comes.

ANGELIC REALM
Angel of the Heaven of Paradise

ANGELIC FUNCTION
To give humankind the gift of its deepest knowing

GIFTS FOR EARTH
It can help you to know your truth;
anchor your awareness in your deepest knowing;
remind you that you always know what is right for you

The Angel of Knowing helps each one of us find and listen to that part of us which always knows. This is the place where we are completely empowered and whole. This is not the function of the rational mind which understands limitations. It is, rather, something in our deepest consciousness which is tuned to the vibrations of the cosmos and is profoundly aware of all things. When we tap into our deep knowing we bypass our mental framework of how reality is supposed to be. We short-circuit our emotions and renounce our negative attitudes towards life. This deep knowing comes from the absolute certainty of who we are, and may manifest itself in voices or pictures or even go beyond images, giving us a direct experience of Self. It is not dependent upon external situations or the imaginings of the mind. It is the strongest possible message, which springs directly from our Soul.

Our sense of knowing may help us realize our purpose in being here on the planet at this time of conflict and strife. This knowing helps us accept what we need to do to let our potential unfold, and make the right choices for our lives. It embraces an awareness that the universe is a benign place and exists to support our being ourselves as fully as possible. This deep knowing is our direct link to the Source. We can offer our prayers to The Angel of Knowing to guide and assist us in increasing our ability to listen within. This angel helps us recognize the state of our moods and emotions, and when we are re-running old tapes about how life has to be for us, it will encourage us to drop the well-worn script and find the positive and joyful.

The Angel of Knowing stands for total clarity. We are given this gift when we have dismissed unhealthy and unwholesome attitudes about ourselves and our brothers and sisters. A part of this knowing is that we are love itself.

Our prayers to The Angel of Knowing can ease our fears and help us open to our centre, which is love and Light. With knowing we can experience certainty and know that we are perfect in the eyes of God.

Thrones: The Angel of

BEING

The Angel of BEING
MY SOUL RESTS IN THE TRUTH
THAT MY BEING IS ETERNAL

The Angel of Being is depicted as the universal symbol of the Self, the mandala. The two chalices encompass both the spiritual and the earthly energy of humanity. The man and woman shown below represent wholeness and individuation. The eye at the top is the symbol of the Heaven of Paradise.

ANGELIC REALM
Angel of the Heaven of Paradise

ANGELIC FUNCTION
To act as God's eyes

GIFTS FOR EARTH
It can help you to touch the depth of your being;
be as a co-creator of the universe;
expand your personal sense of well-being

The Angel of Being blesses us for being mirrors of God's love. It helps transform reality into a vision for ourselves in which we feel loved and supported. It illuminates our awareness that we are a vital part of the creation.

Because we exist as a part of the creation, not separate from it, we are entitled to love, respect and prosperity. The Angel of Being encourages us to know ourselves and to understand that we are, at core, aspects of the Source. This angel gives us assistance to create a simple and fulfilling way of life for ourselves. When we choose joy, love and health, we move towards being co-creators of the universe. The Angel of Being affirms our vision and blesses it. It helps us to create our lives using all the ability we have to draw the good and joyful to us.

We may not see our lives as being particularly creative, yet every negative or positive thought we have draws our experience to us. The Angel of Being is constantly working through our subconscious mind to help us make our reality serve our highest good and greatest joy.

The Angel of Being teaches us about self-acceptance and self-love. It helps us to know our own goodness and the sweetness of our inner nature. Working together with it amounts to accepting ourselves as we are. It means opening our hearts to the vision of what we truly want ourselves to be, an angel in a physical body.

We can pray to The Angel of Being to help us find the courage to enjoy being ourselves. We ask it to help us sort out the magnificence of our essential being from the superficial trappings of the material world. We need to know we are not the car we drive, not the house we live in, the clothes we wear nor the partner we sleep with. Our worth is not dependent on any of these things. We are worthy simply because we exist. We are a unique expression of being, existing beyond the ego-identifications of money, jobs, sex, race, or age. True being is a oneness with the loving and creative spirit within us. May The Angel of Being help us unite with our true self.

Thrones: The Angel of

POWER

The Angel of POWER
THE POWER OF DIVINE LOVE
PROTECTS AND ENFOLDS ME

The Angel of Power is depicted as a swirling mass of energy between the mythical horse Pegasus and a huge whale. One symbolizes transformation of earth-bound matter into spirit; the other the enormity of natural creation. The acorns show that even the smallest kernel has the power for growth and creation.

ANGELIC REALM
Angel of the Heaven of Paradise

ANGELIC FUNCTION
To transform God's love into material form

GIFTS FOR EARTH
It can help you to accept the power of the Source;
acknowledge your own power for transformation;
accept the collective power of humanity for change

The Angel of Power brings us closer to a realization that the power of God lives within each of us. It is our individual work to realize this truth in ourselves and to acknowledge its power. The Angel of Power is there to facilitate this realization and to bring us closer to oneness with the Source.

The power of God's love can be realized as a spiritual concept or experienced as a living reality. The more we make this awareness a living experience, the more we bridge the gap of separation between ourselves and our fellow beings. It is left to each individual to come to know and trust the power within him. The Angel of Power offers us the help we need to make this realization possible.

We can offer up prayers to The Angel of Power to clear our minds of all negativity, which blocks our discovery that God lives within and is not an externalized projection separate from ourselves.

The Angel of Power offers many different ways through which we can come to know the power within us more fully. For some it may be through meditation; for others it may be following a spiritual practice, a particular type of work or occupation; for still others it may come in the form of friendship or fellowship. When we start to follow what attracts us and do what gives us joy, the miracles unfold and we are brought to heights of awareness about what life can be about.

We can offer prayers of gratitude for this power. This helps us to share in the goodness and beauty of creation, knowing we are one with this power and not separate from it. The power of our being increases every time we take a step towards loving ourselves, honouring who we are and respecting the Source of life within us. Every time we honour our beauty and grace and our capacity for gentleness we place ourselves in the light. When we open to our feelings and tell the truth to ourselves about how life is for us at any particular moment, we increase our power and enhance our being. The Angel of Power challenges us at every turn to own our power and live our truth.

Thrones: The Angel of

GLORY

The Angel of **GLORY**
I SING PRAISE AND GLORY TO
THE SOURCE OF ALL LIFE

This angel is shown as a glorious burst of heavenly light. It is seen with some of the very simple things in life which are to be celebrated: the rising sun, a rainbow, children dancing. These are the very basic joys of life, which remind us of the glory of creation.

ANGELIC REALM
Angel of the Heaven of Paradise

ANGELIC FUNCTION
To celebrate the glory of the Divine

GIFTS FOR EARTH
It can help us to celebrate the simple joys of life;
acknowledge all the goodness around us;
give thanks for all that we are

The Angel of Glory helps us to celebrate the endless opportunities for goodness and joy that exist in our lives. It teaches us to be thankful for the beauty and simplicity of life. It actually helps us to take the strain and struggle away from our lives by seeing how simple things can be. This angel tells us that life can be one long celebration if we so choose. It sings praise to the glory of God's wondrous creation. We can tune into this incantation of beauty and joy any time we wish to open our hearts. The splendours of life simply unfold before us. Life then becomes a self-reflecting mirror of love when we see it through eyes of gratitude. It also means that we become rooted in the here-and-now reality of life itself.

We can offer up our prayers to The Angel of Glory to include our thanks in its song of praise and joy to the Source of life. With our hearts open we are blessed; the pleasure we receive in saying 'thank you' for life is the ultimate acknowledgement of life itself. The joy of gratitude nourishes our souls and gives us the deepest feeling of grace. Many years ago a very wise man taught me to say: 'Thank you for all the good things that are happening in my life now.' The more I said it, the more good things happened in my life.

The Angel of Glory helps to raise us above the mundane to a level of celebration about the glory of God and the miracle of creation. To align our energy and awareness with this glory is to be a part of it all. We are each an aspect of the divine principle of creation. It is our own glory which we are celebrating when we open our hearts to the angels. We are reaching the glory of Self and honouring the Divine when we love ourselves.

— ✱ —

Chapter Three

HOW TO USE THE ANGEL CARDS

Praise be to all the angels for ever

TOBIT, 11:15

The angel oracle is designed to be user-friendly and simple. It is a model of the love and perfection of the Angelic Realms, and offers you a special relationship to aspects of yourself you may not have been aware of before. It can bring you closer to the angels who guide and protect you in your path through this life.

HOW TO PREPARE THE CARDS

There are some aspects to using the cards which you may care to know before you start. These simple actions help the cards radiate a strong quality of love and devotion. They keep the energy around the cards clean and purified.

Consider keeping your cards in a special place in your home where your energy is calm and serene. You may wish to wrap them in a piece of silk or find a special box for them. Think about putting them on or near your meditation shrine or next to your bed. Before using them, light a candle and burn incense to purify the space around you. Angels thrive in a beautiful atmosphere and can contact you much more easily if you are calm and your space is purified.

You may wish to sit silently in meditation, holding the cards in your hands and being with the angels in whatever way feels best for you. You will certainly develop your own unique rituals when using the cards.

The angels will always encourage you to do what feels right for you. You may want flowers near by, or wish to play soft music while you lay the cards out on a beautiful piece of cloth. The composer Marcia Hamm has created some divinely inspired music which I often play when working with THE ANGEL ORACLE. There are some beautiful music tapes which are gentle and inspiring and can help you open up your heart to the angels.

ASKING THE ORACLE QUESTIONS

You can ask the angels any questions which are important to you, though these should not be framed as if to receive a simple 'yes/no' response. The Sample Readings below will show you the best way to frame a question. The angels will help you find clarity and understanding and help you to increase your intuitive abilities.

If you find that you are not getting the answers you wish but are receiving information that may confuse you, 'step back' from the cards for a while and reflect on the answers you have received. It takes a peaceful spirit to understand fully the revelatory nature of these cards, or any other divination tools for that matter. Be calm and gentle and let the informa-tion unfold. Angels cannot be forced, nor will they tolerate demands. If you truly do not understand the answers that come up, ask the angels to please clarify your reading so that you can understand. Give yourself time to reflect on the information you are receiving. Sometimes things become clear after a night's sleep or through a dream.

You may wish to write down your readings in an Angel Notebook and consider what information has been revealed to you. Over time you will be able to see how this information has unfolded. This will help you to trust the quality of the love which is being given to you through these cards.

CHOOSING A CARD SPREAD

Look carefully at the different card spreads and readings which can be consulted for THE ANGEL ORACLE (see pages 102–109). Select the one which best covers your needs. Your question may be fairly straightfor-ward, in which case you will only need one of the simple readings (see the Single Card and the Past, Present and Future readings for an example). If you require a more complex answer you can choose a more intricate spread from the selection given (see the Sacred Cross reading for an exam-ple). THE ANGEL ORACLE is designed to cover a wide variety of eventualities and to give you as thorough a reading as possible.

The angels bring only positive energy into your life. These cards let you look at a situation or a personal issue in a clear and positive way.

Trust your Higher Self to guide you and to gain access to the angels in the truest way it knows how.

INTERPRETATION OF THE CARDS

You can interpret the cards at any level you choose. You can approach them in as light-hearted or as serious a manner as you like, but either way these cards are a powerful key to your deepest emotional and spiritual processes.

If you wish to have full value from THE ANGEL ORACLE, give real consideration to the questions you pose to the angels. Ask for a reading in the name of your highest good and greatest joy. Meditate for a few moments with the cards in your hands and hold the question you want to ask in your mind while you shuffle and cut them. You will get the best possible reading by giving your question attention and focus. To get the deepest and richest interpretation from THE ANGEL ORACLE, focus your awareness on the card and ask yourself what this means for you in your life right now. Situations change as we change, and the more you can allow the angels to offer their love and healing the more easily and the faster the insights will come to you.

Single Card reading

This is an instant reading when you want a fast, definitive answer to a question about a situation or emotional issue. Simply shuffle the cards and cut them three ways with your left hand, holding your question in your mind. Draw a card from anywhere in the deck, or take a card from on top of the deck.

Trust yourself to choose whatever card really draws you. Let this card represent the angel's answer to your question. Spend a moment reflecting how this angel can assist you with your question. Let the energy come into your consciousness. You will know what the angels are telling you.

SAMPLE READING Susie wanted to have a single card reading for a decision she had made about moving to a new house. She asked the Oracle if this was right for her. The card she drew was The Angel of Serenity from the Powers in the Heaven of Creation. She interpreted this to mean that moving was a good decision and that she would enjoy serenity in her new abode.

Ying/Yang spread (two cards)

Any time you are faced with a double-bind situation, or find yourself confronting a powerful paradox, this spread can be of help to you. It is designed for you to see through to the polarity and dual nature of a perplexing situation or emotional issue. Sometimes we want to know the two sides of any situation and this spread helps us to see the negative and positive, the male and female, the dark and the light principles unfolding in our lives.

Shuffle the cards and cut them three times with your left hand, holding your question in your mind. Now ask for a Yin card which represents the feminine/receptive or negative polarity of your situation. Place that card on your left side.

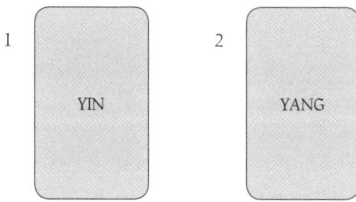

Yin/Yang spread

Now ask for a card which represents the opposite, Yang/masculine or positive polarity of your situation. This card should be placed on your right side.

If you need another point of view draw a card from the deck and let it represent the neutral aspect of your situation, one that blends its two opposite poles.

Past, Present, Future spread (three cards)

Shuffle the cards and cut them with your left hand, holding your question in your mind. Draw a card, which represents the past. Place it on your left side. Draw a second card, representing the present. Place that in the middle between the past and future spaces. Draw a third card, which represents the future. Place this on your right side.

This should give you a sense of continuity, transformation and resolution to whatever your situation is. Remember when you work with the future tense to trust in the angels that everything will emerge for your highest good and greatest joy.

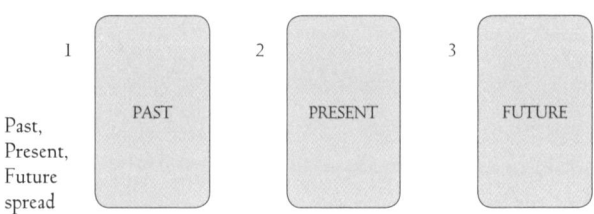

1		2		3
	PAST		PRESENT		FUTURE

Past,
Present,
Future
spread

SAMPLE READING Jason asked THE ANGEL ORACLE about his future with his present employer. He did a Past, Present, Future spread, which gave him in the past The Angel of Trust, from the Virtues in the Heaven of Creation; The Archangel Raphael in the present; and The Guardian Angel of Maturity in the future, both from the Heaven of Form. He interpreted this to mean that The Angel of Trust represented all his aspirations about the job. He was very happy in the early stages of his work and felt a lot of self-worth in being chosen for the job over other candidates. He understood The Archangel Raphael, who represents the healing aspect of the Divine, to stand for the healing that took place while he took on the responsibility of his new job. He had left home, set up his own place, worked successfully for five years and healed his lack of confidence in himself to get on in life. He read The Guardian Angel of Maturity to mean that he would continue to grow through his work.

The reading helped Jason to feel confident that he was on the right path, and was really doing the very best for himself. It renewed his faith in his work, and it also gave him an added incentive to be creative in his job.

Four-function Psychological spread (four cards)

This spread represents the four functions of your psychological make-up: intellect, feelings, intuition and sensation. The cards in this spread can also stand for the four aspects of any situation, and can give you a deeper sense of the different dimensions of your own situation.

Shuffle the cards and cut them three times with your left hand, holding the question clearly in your mind. Draw the cards one at a time and place them in the order shown in the diagram. The left one represents your intellect; the right one your feelings; the top one your intuition; and the bottom one sensation.

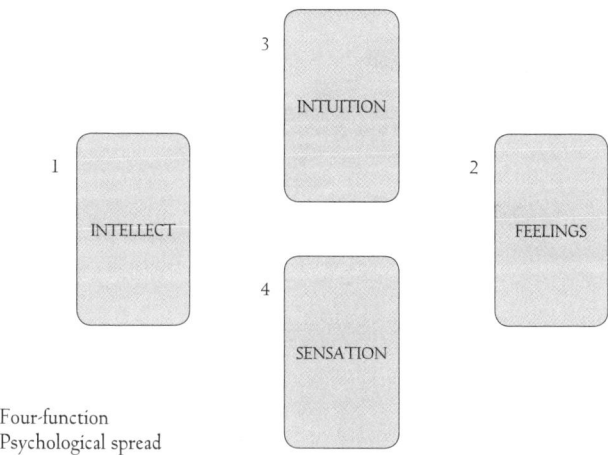

Four-function
Psychological spread

When you have laid out all the cards, look at each one carefully to see what information the angels are giving you about these functions. Are there parts of yourself that may need more attention and to which you might wish to give more love and attention? Let the angels tell you how they can assist you.

Tree of Life spread (five cards)

This is a reading which takes into account the needs of your Higher Self as well as the underlying influences which are working at an unconscious level in your situation. The spread contains the past, present and future readings but also has an extra dimension to help you see the deeper forces which are at work.

Shuffle the cards and cut them three times with your left hand. Hold your question in your mind. Draw the cards and lay them down in the order shown in the diagram. The top left one represents the past; the top centre one your present situation; the top right one the future. The card below the centre one is your Higher Self, and is the aspect of your psyche which creates your external reality, forming situations which allow you to grow and develop as a spiritual being. The bottom card represents the underlying influences which are active in your life at the present moment and which are working on the situation you have asked about.

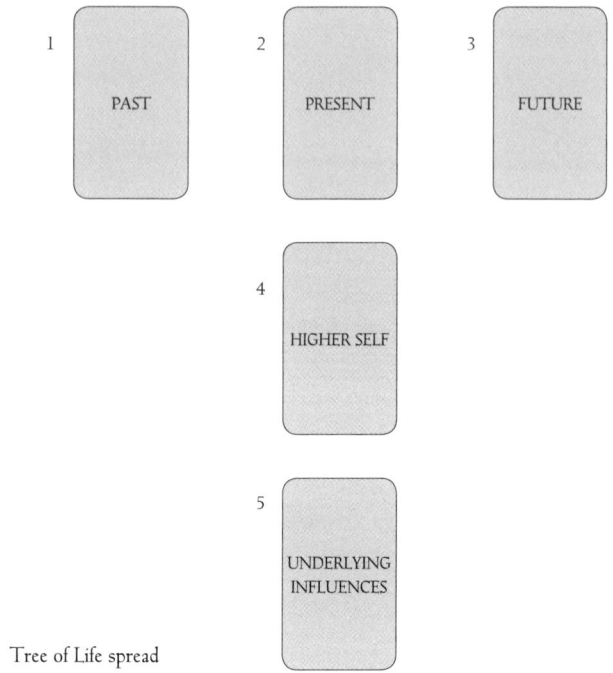

Tree of Life spread

Sacred Cross spread (six cards)

This spread works to give you a good look at any situation. It is of particular benefit in helping you to see a question from different points of view. It can give you a very good perspective on any situation where you want to see all the challenges as well as the best possible outcome.

Shuffle the cards and cut them three times with your left hand. Hold your question in your mind. Draw six cards, one at a time, following the diagram. The first one, which goes to form the right side of the cross, represents the past; the second, forming the left side of the cross, is the future. The third card, at the bottom of the cross, is the foundation card and represents the cornerstone of the situation you are asking about.

The next card, representing your Higher Self, goes directly above the previous card. It stands for your highest good and greatest joy. The fifth card, which goes above the previous one, represents the challenges that face you in the situation. The angels are sharing with you what you will be dealing with as you grow and develop. The last card goes above the previous one and represents the best possible outcome in the situation.

Sacred Cross spread

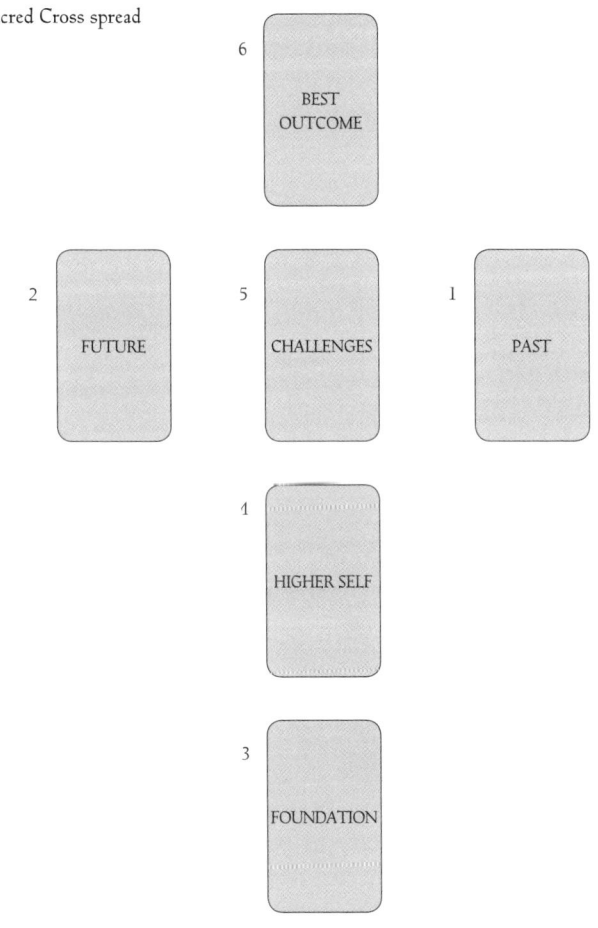

6 — BEST OUTCOME

2 — FUTURE

5 — CHALLENGES

1 — PAST

4 — HIGHER SELF

3 — FOUNDATION

SAMPLE READING Emma was having problems in her relationship. She asked for a reading which could give her some insight into her life and would indicate specifically if her relationship was going to last.

She chose to do the Sacred Cross reading and this was the result: she drew The Archangel Metatron in the place of the past, and The Angel Prince of the North to represent the future, both from the Heaven of Form. The third card she drew was from the Virtues in the Heaven of Creation, The Angel of Faith in the place of the foundation card.

The card she picked for the Higher Self was from the Powers, also in the Heaven of Creation, The Angel of Peace. The fifth card, which represents the challenge she faced, was one of the Seraphim in the Heaven of Paradise, The Angel of Eternal Love. And for the last card, which represents the best outcome, she selected another Power, The Angel of Harmony.

The interpretation she chose for herself was that Metatron expressed her need for recognition, which was a deep, underlying cause for her at the beginning of her relationship. He is the Archangel who represents our good deeds. Emma felt she did a lot of rescuing in the beginning with her boyfriend, in the hope of being recognized by him as a good person. She was not very sure of herself and was always trying to do help-ful things.

The Angel Prince of the North, which was in the place of the future card, represents the psychological function of thinking. She interpreted this to mean that she would need to develop her capacity to think for herself in the relationship and not be so dependent on her partner making decisions for her. She understood this to mean that she needed to think about what she wanted from her life.

The card which is the foundation card and represents the Higher Self was one of the Virtues, The Angel of Faith. She took this to mean that, even if there were rough patches in the relationship, even if she and her partner separated, she needed to have faith that her life was unfolding for her highest good.

She drew The Angel of Eternal Love from the Seraphim, in the place of the life challenge facing her. She understood this to mean that, no matter what happened, she recognized that her partner was a feature in her development and that the love they shared would always be a part of her life.

She drew from the Powers The Angel of Harmony for the best possible outcome. She realized when she drew this card that she and her partner were not sharing a harmonious life together, and that this was what she really wanted from her relationship.

She felt that the reading gave her a deeper understanding of her own internal process of development and showed her in which direction she could hope to develop herself. She said she felt remarkably calm at the end of the reading and it alleviated a lot of her anxiety about her relationship.

The Zodiac spread (thirteen cards)

This spread uses the twelve houses of the Zodiac. It provides a background for you to see where you are in terms of holistic life development. It looks at everything from money and relationships to what stage you are at in your spiritual growth.

The Zodiac spread

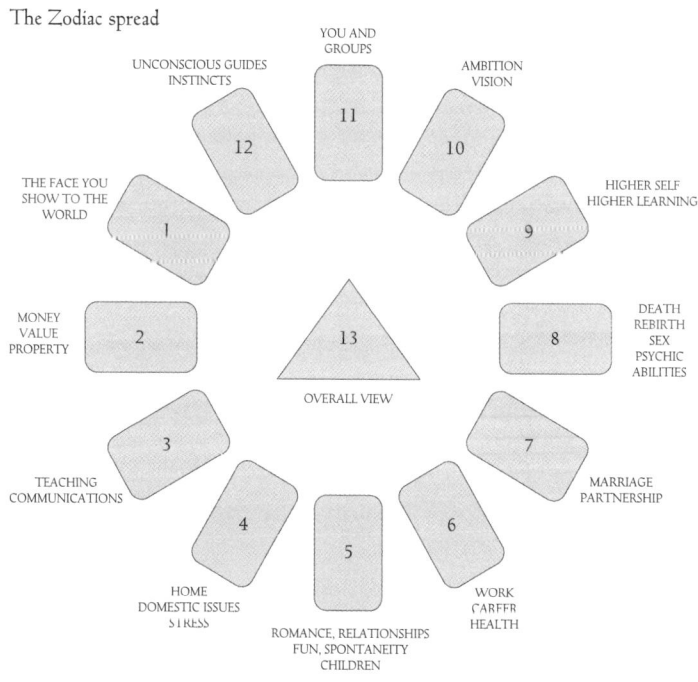

Before you shuffle the cards you may wish to meditate by sitting still in a comfortable position with your eyes closed, reflecting on your life. Shuffle the cards and cut them three times with your left hand. Hold your question as you draw a card while you ask the angels for the best possible reading for you right now in your life. Place the card in the position of the house of the Zodiac it represents. The first card will go in the first house, the second card in the second house, and so on. The diagram illustrates what each house represents. The thirteenth card gives an overall view of your life as it stands now.

CONCLUSION

Whether you use one card or a dozen, the messages from the angels are there for your illumination as well as your pleasure. Try to remember the angels wish you only joy and peace in your life. They offer all the possibilities of the love we seek with the least amount of struggle or pain. Create the opportunity for them to bring joy into your life. Allow these cards to act as a healing tool for you to find your highest good and greatest joy.

THE ANGEL ORACLE is a unique gift from the realm of the angels. It can give you guidance and enhance your development as the spiritual being you are. Work with the angels through the cards to develop your own sense of what is right and good for you. Open your heart to the good that can be channelled through you. A young friend of mine, Terri Logan, aged twelve, told me that she loved angels because they were absolutely safe. She, like many people today, has a very sensitive nature and is in touch with realms of awareness which are deeply moving and spiritual.

Ease your way into the reality of angels through the cards. Trust your own inner nature to unfold for you as you become comfortable meditating with the angel cards. The advice and help you can gain from working with the cards may help you directly to transform aspects of your life that give you anxiety or unhappiness.

We seek information through our intuition, which allows us to make conscious and healthy decisions. The angels are always helping you in your life. THE ANGEL ORACLE is a visible link to that world of support, love and guidance which awaits your conscious recognition.

SUGGESTED READING

Boros, Ladislaus: *Angels and Men*, Search Press, London, 1974

Burnham, Sophy: *A Book of Angels*, Ballantine Books, New York, 1990

Connolly, David: *In Search of Angels*, Perigee Books, Putnam Publishing, New York, 1993

Davidson, Gustav: *A Dictionary of Angels*, The Free Press, Macmillan, New York, 1967

Mallasz, Gitta: *Talking with Angels*, Diamon Verlag, Switzerland, 1992

Moolenburgh, H. C.: *A Handbook of Angels*, C. W. Daniels Company, Saffron Walden, 1988

Moolenburgh, H. C.: *Meetings with Angels*, C. W. Daniels Company, Saffron Walden, 1992

Steiner, Rudolf: *The Spiritual Hierarchies*, Anthroposophic Press, New York, 1970

Synnestvedt, Sig: *The Essential Swedenborg*, The Swedenborg Foundation Inc., New York, 1970

Szekely, Edmond Bordeaux: *The Gospel of the Essenes*, C. W. Daniels Company, Saffron Walden, 1979

Taylor, Terry Lynn: *Messengers of Light*, H. J. Kramer, Inc., Tiburon, California, 1990

Taylor, Terry Lynn: *Guardians of Hope*, H. J. Kramer, Inc., Tiburon, California, 1992

Taylor, Terry Lynn: *Creating with the Angels*, H. J. Kramer, Inc., Tiburon, California, 1993

Acknowledgements

My deepest thanks to the angels who watch over me and who guided me to create the Oracle. I know that in the course of writing this book there have been many events and circumstances in which I have been assured of the tremendous love and support they bring. My thanks to Susan Mears, my agent, for her ideas for the Oracle. The team at Eddison Sadd Limited have been both understanding and respectful of this project, and a real pleasure to work with. My thanks to Ian Jackson for his guidance and to Nick Eddison for his ability to realize the project. I would like to thank Elisabeth Ingles for editing the text and Warren Maddill for his beautiful artwork.

My love and thanks to Charlie Moritz for reading the script and giving help and support throughout. Thanks to his father, Ernest, who found many of the beautiful Jewish prayers quoted in the Oracle. Among my friends, special thanks to Lady Mary Jardine, and to Dale Culliford and Patrick Gundry-White for their excellent weekly Alexander Technique lessons and for providing the right books at the right time to help my research on angels.

My love to the spirit of my Grandmother who I know watches over me, and to my mother and sister who rest with the angels. God bless us all.

Contact Me

For details of my seminars, workshops and other
publications available, please visit my websites at:

- www.lifeenergymedicine.com
- www.ambikawauters.com